DATE DUE

Haim Hazan is a leading specialist on old age in anthropology, and he has published several monographs on particular communities of old people. The present book is a general essay on the realities of old age, as it is experienced, as opposed to the ideas about the old that are current in western societies. It argues that the construction of this world by outsiders is inevitably affected by deeply ingrained social attitudes and structures, such as the spatial segregation of the aged as a population, and the fear of death with which they are associated. By approaching the subject from a social constructionist perspective, and drawing on a variety of detailed ethnographic accounts of the old, the author describes a unique and nuanced social world. This is a sophisticated and original book, which should have a significant impact on a field still dominated by a 'social problems' approach.

Old age: constructions and deconstructions

Themes in the Social Sciences

Editors: John Dunn, Jack Goody, Geoffrey Hawthorn

Old age: constructions and deconstructions

HAIM HAZAN

Tel-Aviv University

CAMBRIDGE
UNIVERSITY PRESS

Published by the Press Syndicate of the University of Cambridge
The Pitt Building, Trumpington Street, Cambridge, CB2 1RP
40 West 20th Street, New York, NY 10011–4211, USA
10 Stamford Road, Oakleigh, Melbourne 3166, Australia

Cambridge University Press, 1994

First published 1994

Printed in Great Britain at the University Press, Cambridge

A catalogue record for this book is available from the British Library

Library of Congress cataloguing in publication data
Hazan, Haim
Constructions and deconstructions of old age / Haim Hazan.
p.   cm.
Includes bibliographical references
ISBN (invalid) 0 521 44424 4. – ISBN 0 521 44748–8 (pbk.)
1. Aged. 2. Old age. I. Title.
HQ1061.H378   1994
305.26 – dc20   93–8058   CIP

ISBN 0 521 44240 0 hardback
ISBN 0 521 44748 8 paperback

If youngsters say to you: construct, and elders – demolish, demolish; since construction by youth is deconstruction and deconstruction by elders is construction. *(The Talmud: Megilah, p. 31)*

Contents

Acknowledgements

A book such as this owes its scope and content to the intersection of many academic disciplines – in our case: social gerontology, socio-cultural anthropology and sociology – and to the inspiration of literature, art and philosophy. It would be a futile exercise to track down the various paths leading to this end-product and to depict the mosaic of ideas and associations composing it. Furthermore, I claim sole responsibility for the nature and the presentation of the message and hence pointing at specific names, trends, studies or schools would not do them justice. I therefore reserve the offerings of gratitude to those who were directly involved in shaping the following pages.

The production of this book was facilitated by the assistance of several persons. I am particularly grateful to Mr D. Glanz, Mr A. Raz and Ms B. Metzger who were immensely helpful in various stages of preparing the manuscript. Special thanks are due to Dr Edgar Siskin, Director of the Jerusalem Institute for Anthropological Studies, The Faculty of Social Sciences in Tel-Aviv University, and the Bar Ilan Brookdale Program in Applied Gerontology, and the Brookdale Institute of Gerontology and Adult Human Development in Jerusalem, whose financial support was invaluable to the project. Professor Don Handelman offered insightful comments which greatly contributed to the development of parts of the argument. The considerable patience and encouragement extended by Dr Jessica Kuper of Cambridge University Press were much appreciated throughout. The helpful hand and the understanding ear lent to me by my wife, Mercia, proved to be a significant contribution to the successful completion of the book.

Acknowledgements

At this stage a personal note is in order. My interest in the existential enigma of ageing was bound up with the untimely death of three members of my family who did not reach old age in any sense of the parameters of this book. Thus I would like to dedicate the spirit of this book to the memory of my parents, Sima and David Hazan, and my father-in-law Sydney Keye.

Introduction: towards knowledge of old age

Human experience is shaped by human constructs. Through a complex set of social arrangements, cultural codes are deciphered, negotiated and sustained as conceptual devices for interpreting situations, values and norms. These devices inform a structure of social knowledge which extends throughout all areas of life and permeates the products, tangible and intangible, of human consciousness. Actions and interactions, thoughts and utterances, artefacts and works of art are the language in which such social knowledge is articulated. Concepts, therefore, are not merely abstract reflections but are deeply embedded in both the form and content of everything human.[1]

Social knowledge is formulated and acquired through the structural language of distinctions (Bourdieu 1984). By setting up contrasting conceptual categories we bring a sense of order to otherwise unfathomable experience. The cultural language pertaining to the old is one instance of such categorization. In modern secular society, the encounter with the elderly is experienced as tangential to the inevitable encounter with the boundary between life and death. Unlike class, ethnic, racial or even gender-based distinctions, the boundary between life and death is a perennial human preoccupation. Ageing, as one of the major markers of that fine existential line, calls for constant clarification and reclassification.

Knowledge about ageing is peculiar; alongside matters of life and death it embraces notions about dependency and autonomy, body and soul, and paradoxes emanating from irreconcilable tensions between images of the old, their own will and desires, and the

1

facilities offered to them. The world of the aged is supposedly rendered intelligible by means of widely available information, and through the professional interpretive expertise of welfare workers, doctors, nurses, psychologists, and social policy makers this information is transformed into know-how – the measures designed to handle the problems ascribed to the aged and used to plan old-age homes, day centres, welfare facilities and financial benefits on their behalf. This marriage between information and know-how is, however, rarely informed by knowledge of the matter at hand. The socio-cultural construction of knowledge of ageing disguises an undercurrent of fear and anxiety.

Knowledge rests on understanding[2] of social boundaries and systems of accountability; it constitutes and reflects the world we witness and experience and the sets of rules, codes and obligations with which we were aligned (Douglas 1973). Information, know-how and knowledge are usually mutually reinforcing. For example, conceptions of the relationship between adults and their children and the desirable position of the latter within society provide the basis for a cultural code regarding childhood according to which certain information about children is given prominence and frameworks are established for socializing them into their milieu (Ariès 1965). Again, the management of disease rests on symbolic (albeit culturally variable) distinctions between health and illness; images of warfare underpin the 'fight' against the invader of the body, and disease and death are portrayed in terms of military defeat (Sontag 1989). In both these instances, there is a relative congruence between information, know-how, and knowledge. In the case of ageing this is not the case.

Generally speaking, knowledge, rather than consisting of the data at our disposal, is shaped by perceptions, beliefs, rationalizations and other non-rational forms of imagery. When we speak of knowledge, then, what we have in mind is in effect images of knowledge. In the case of old age, information about the aged is used, wittingly or otherwise, to sustain the social position it reflects. Thus, age structure, income, housing and epidemiology are all constructs of know-how that seek to establish linkages between the aged and the facilities, budgets and resources allocated to them. The cultural and existential origins of knowledge concerning the old, however, are often implicit. Communication about ageing does not necessarily rely on communication with the ageing, much less communication amongst the aged. Most of the professional literature on ageing is aimed at the know-how-oriented reader, whose interest is in information about the state of the elderly as an object. Only a smattering of research is dedicated to deciphering the world of old people as subjects, and even less of this work attempts to understand the ways in which knowledge about ageing is produced and reproduced. This book is one such endeavour.

The acquisition and construction of shared knowledge about so charged and ambiguous a domain of human experience are confounded by the double-bind of two conflicting modes of reference to ageing. On the one hand, a host of socio-psychological forces operate to remove aged people from the rest of society and to assign them to a symbolic and physical enclave. On the other hand, the awareness that most of us will eventually occupy that enclave is ever-present. The sense of continuity of self is betrayed by the fear of 'being there', and the perception of the indivisibility of the self is challenged by the awareness of finitude. Hence, the existential origins of knowledge about ageing engender a multifaceted corpus of conceptions, beliefs and attitudes, the kaleidoscopic character of which reflects ever-changing personal and social needs. Social scientists intent on disentangling this complex must not only be held accountable for deciphering socio-cultural models of ageing but must also be prepared to examine the academic analysis itself.

The attempt to elicit specific social knowledge is inevitably self-subversive. The necessary high degree of generalization, verging on simplification, may lead to loss of details of the texture and design of social life. Self-awareness and reflexivity produce the springboard from which to make the quantum leap from the particular to the general. Philosophy, literature, music, the fine arts and popular culture furnish the social sciences with insights into the concepts they set out to understand and develop. Ethnicity, family, role, tribe and tradition, projected onto reality and given ontological status, become analytic devices. These concepts, straddling the worlds of researcher and research subjects, fieldworkers and field, are a uniquely intriguing property of the social sciences.

Any attempt to formulate a model of ageing is further confounded

by the poverty of reflective material on the subject, the tendentious-
ness of the body of research on ageing, and, above all, the multivocal and even demonic role played by ageing in our consciousness.
Caught between empathy and awe, intellectual attraction and social
barriers, students of later life face major difficulties in gaining access
to knowledge. The myriad personal, ethical, existential and cultural
issues involved in this quest may provoke a radical rethinking of
social categories, symbolic boundaries and taken-for-granted reality.

The possible ways of acquiring such knowledge may be placed
along a continuum, at one end of which lie attempts to approach the
assumed unique universe of the aged by tapping the personal
experience of being old. In this approach, in-depth interviewing,
diaries, and verbal accounts of the aged are taken as windows into
their inner world. Titles such as *The View in Winter* (Blythe 1979) and
Number Our Days (Myerhoff 1978a), indicate a desire to remove
social masks and reach the unadulterated self-awareness of the
aged. At the other end of the continuum, the quest for knowledge
about old age rejects direct accounts of personal meaning in favour
of recognized analytic concepts. In this approach, titles such as
Socialization to Old Age (Rosow 1974), *The Cultural Context of Ageing*
(Sokolovsky 1990), and *Dimensions: Aging, Culture, and Health* (Fry
1981) are stripped of emotive, critical, or tendentious connotations.
The distinction between these two approaches may be described as
'experience-near', 'experience-distant' (Geertz 1979): while the
former draws on the language of the people under study, the latter
develops a detached terminology which endows the work with an
aura of objectivity. Both perspectives have pitfalls: while reported
experience fails to achieve objective validity, 'value-free' terms of
reference lack credibility.

This book explores the relationship between the experience of the
old and the concepts developed to explain it, and proposes a
metalanguage capable of reflecting upon both. Moving from a
critical comparison of experience-near with experience-distant
approaches, I shall identify a set of constructs which are intentio-
nally not experience-oriented but structural and acontextual. The
assumption underlying this approach is that the two separate ways
of constructing old age as an object of knowledge – old age as a form
of self-awareness and the social (including analytic) conception of

old age – may be attributed to differences in perspective on the boundary between life and death, as construed respectively by those on its verge and those desperate to avoid it.

Since the subject at hand is variegated, any endeavour to understand it must employ a variety of discourses. Whereas research in the socio-cultural domain usually involves commitment to a particular theoretical approach, the case of ageing does not lend itself to any such commitment. On the contrary, the sharp disjunctions between levels of discussion produce incongruent perspectives on ageing and call for an interpretive model appropriate to its intricacies. Rather than being subjected to arbitrarily selected conceptual models, the production of a metalanguage about ageing will draw upon the dialogue engendered by competing explanatory models. Though much comparative evidence will be drawn from pre-industrial societies, the discourse on ageing developed herein is drawn from the experience of modern or post-modern living.

Because the socio-cultural construction of ageing is shaped by cultural ideologies as well as by socio-economic concerns, the temptation to interpret it in terms of its socio-cultural context is strong. The holistic approach of anthropological inquiry is based on the (common-sense) notion of context as a locus of unity, converging perspectives, complementariness and order. A commitment to context is inappropriate, however, for addressing the highly fragmented conditions of growing and being old in our society. The multiple realities inhabited by the individual and the diversity of available socio-cultural life-styles make any use of a unified context irrelevant and even misleading. Furthermore, while most socio-anthropological discourse assumes a necessary link between self and observed behaviour, amongst the aged separate domains of existence – personal experience and social constructions of old age – may co-exist. Because these two domains do not necessarily inform each other, they do not produce a recognizable, unified context. Some of the forces that shape the lives of elderly people – for example, accumulated life experience and existential problems stemming from the natural process of deterioration coupled with socially induced losses – do not in fact originate in their immediate context at all. The combination of these factors weighs heavily on the lives of the aged, and their highly divergent nature serves to weaken the determining role of common socio-cultural features. The relative irrelevance of context in the lives of the old is further reinforced by the perception of the social category of the old as a 'problem' for which 'solutions' are to be sought in the engineering of specially designed environments that ignore differences among the elderly inhabitants and efface their past. The irrelevance of context makes it difficult to understand ageing, the more so because it is debatable whether understanding can be expected from phenomenological and psychological perspectives. What is needed is a socio-cultural paradigm concerning the 'intersubjective' construction of experience and particularly of the self-contradictory construct of old age.

Underlying this book is the conviction that old age is a unique case study in the hermeneutic process whereby the social codes used in the construction of a conceptual category are the subject of study of social sciences that are themselves built upon those very codes. Eschewing context, on the one hand, and subjectivity, on the other, the study of ageing as a social entity must focus on the interstices between various spheres of knowledge. The particular kind of knowledge that arises out of the gaps, inconsistencies, and incongruities intrinsic to the cultural perception of the old, requires an appropriate language, one which addresses differences and contradictions rather than coherence and compatibility.

This book, therefore, can be read in two ways. First, it can be regarded as a construction, providing a critical overview and a practical guide to the theoretical field generally known as the sociology of ageing. Secondly, and as a logical consequence of both its ethnographic evidence and its critical diagnosis, it can be seen as a deconstruction, an alternative to these sociological theories. Structurally it consists of two contrasting parts, respectively referring to old age as a socio-cultural object among the non-old and to the ways in which the old construct their own world. Part I presents four ways of representing old age. Chapter 1 describes knowledge of old age as embedded in common linguistic usage and demonstrates how such locutions express social segregation and erect barriers of ignorance. It goes on to describe the various ways in which societies handle the presence within them of the category of the old. Chapter 2 maps the symbolic codes generated to reflect and sustain the ambivalences and ambiguities inherent in the cultural position of the old. Chapter 3 turns to the incumbents of the category of the old and unravels some of the stratagems engaged in by the elderly, as individuals and in groups, to sustain a 'roleless' social role and to survive a self-subversive existence. Chapter 4 examines abortive attempts on the part of scholars of old age to formulate acontextual, universal theories of ageing. Abandoning these four discourses, Part II develops a foundation for an alternative model of old age. Chapter 5 discusses social control as it is manifested in the organization of the life cycle, and Chapter 6 describes the structures of meaning entailed in the intricate symbolization of life and death. The complex relations between control and meaning in old age set the socio-cultural scene for an understanding of the unique universe of the old. Chapter 7 studies the contours of this universe through its unique construction of time, space and the self, arguing that the central problem confronted by elderly persons is that they exist in a world of disordered time, a world in which time is fragmented, anomic, and unruly. Understanding this phenomenon may enable us to comprehend ageing in a new way. The book concludes with some reflections on the emergent sociological properties of this proposal and some suggestions for an old-age-based self-knowledge for the non-old.

Contemporary culture consists of a *mélange* of symbolic spheres and semantic areas whose interlinkages are contingent upon assumptions about inconsistent meanings and deconstructed identities. Each of the discourses contained in this book constructs a self-sufficient vocabulary pertaining to a given area of socio-cultural knowledge. Underlying the transition to the concluding chapter is the shift from taken-for-granted sociological and social references to ageing and the old to a full-fledged reflective awareness of the subject. Viewing old age in terms of its epistemological properties, the argument returns to experience-based first-order language on ageing by way of its fundamental guiding principles rather than through personally slanted contents and culturally imprinted attitudes.

The scope and nature of this book cannot do justice to the rapidly growing corpus of socio-anthropological research on ageing. The empirical interjections that appear at four points in the course of the discussion are designed to provide an ethnographic reflection on the theoretical ideas previously presented. Apart from the material that follows this introduction, all the data are from my own studies (see, e.g., 1980a, 1981, 1984, 1985, 1990). The first of these ethnographic reflections offers contrasting examples of the production of ageing-related knowledge, one a first-hand account of the experience of being old, and the other an academically phrased presentation of old age. The second ethnographic reflection, which follows the third chapter, is a case study of life in an old-age home in which some aspects of the social construction of old age are apparent. The second part of the book is illustrated by a further case study which attests to the differences in temporal perspectives, spatial organization, and types of selfhood between the two objects of knowledge of old age. The conclusions are illuminated by two products of the construction of old age – a cultural configuration and a document produced by elderly people themselves. The contrast between these two texts well illustrates that the split between the world of the elderly and conceptions about old age remains fundamentally unbridgeable.

ETHNOGRAPHIC REFLECTION: TOUCHING UPON EXPERIENCE

The English poet, writer, and literary critic, Ronald Blythe, has undertaken to discover the country of the aged, and in *The View in Winter* (1979) he presents adaptations of life stories told him by the people he has met. Quoting 'the schoolmaster', aged 84, he writes (pp. 226–8):

> Old age doesn't necessarily mean that one is entirely old – *all* old, if you follow me. It doesn't mean that for many people, which is why it is so very difficult. It is complicated by the retention of a lot of one's youth in an old body. I tend to look upon other men as *old men* – and not include myself. It is not vanity; it is just that it is still natural for me to be young in some respects. What is generally assumed to have happened to a man in his eighties has not happened to me. The generalizations which go with my age don't apply. Yet I resent it all in some ways, this being very old, yes, I resent it. I have lost most of my physical strength, and once I was strong and loved doing physical work. I am not used to the loss of strength, and I object when many

8

tasks show that they are now beyond me. I cannot quite believe that I can't carry this or turn, or hold the other. This old part of me worries the young part of me. It could be that it would be better to be all old. I think that De La Mare's got the confusion in a nutshell. His poem, 'A Portrait', says it all. I read it often now and find that the cap fits.

... King Lear said, 'When the mind's free the body's delicate', and that is true. My mind is very free now but it isn't wandering. It is definite and active in all directions. I feel so alive but my muscles tell me otherwise. I resent it a little and it's no good pretending that I don't. There has been a great loss of confidence. I'm not certain about anything now. There are great losses and small gains. I don't think that you grow in wisdom when you're old but I do think that, in some respects, you do grow in understanding. The very old are often as tolerant as the young. The young haven't yet adopted certain formal codes and the very old have seen through them or no longer need them. I used to think this and believe that but I don't now. I circumscribe my wants. Few are as important as they once were and they tend to lie quiet unless disturbed. They disturb me when I go out of my way to stimulate them – only then.

While the writer here introduces the narrator in terms of his age and profession, the narrator identifies himself through an articulation of his own grapplings with these two rough signifiers. His subtle rendition of the components of age and identity, coupled with his literary informed pursuit of self-knowledge, turns the schoolmaster's testimony into a dialogue with the writer and his readers. Emerging from first-hand experience, the text reflects a multitude of personal universes of meaning, ranging from physical sensations to the sublime domains of philosophy and literature.

In contrast, the table of contents of a volume entitled *Handbook of Aging and the Social Sciences* (Binstock and Shanas 1985) is a fine example of the attempt to preserve the distance of so-called scientific language from the categories enunciated by the subject of its study:

Part One: The Social Aspects of Aging
  1. Scope, Concepts, and Methods in the Study of Aging
  2. Age and the Life Course

Part Two: Aging and Social Structure
  3. Aging and World-Wide Population Change
  4. Societal Development and Aging

The calculated vocabulary is evident. Areas which cannot be addressed without resorting to the language of experience, such as interpersonal relationships, change, and death, are either phrased in highly formal terms such as 'dyadic relationship', and 'non-institutionalized roles' or expressed in terms of disciplines that traditionally handle matters of the soul and spirit. Terms such as 'caring', 'denial' and 'fear' serve as intermediary concepts for transposing human experience into detached analysis and vice versa.

Part I

Representations of ageing: languages about old age

1

The social trap: the language of separation

Everyday rhetorics reflect spheres of taken-for-granted knowledge about the world. That knowledge, symbolically expressed and inter-actively maintained, preserves social boundaries and cultural classifications. The nomenclature of ageing is a device for introducing order into an inherently ambiguous human condition. Designed to make meaningful the meaningless and describe the indescribable, it uses codes of sequestration and separation to construct a wall around ageing. Thus, while facilitating communication by creating shared attitudes, it also serves to perpetuate misunderstanding.

The term 'aged' not only describes individuals but also is used as a collective noun, and once individuals are identified as 'old' they are perceived exclusively as such. Even the alternative terms, some-times used to soften the negative connotations of the word 'old', 'the elderly', 'older persons', 'senior citizens', 'elders' or 'old age pensioners' – all serve to stigmatize the aged. Such linguistic gen-eralizations cannot be justified on either logical or empirical grounds. The label 'old' may be used, for example, to describe both persons in their sixties who are still physically active and fully capable of functioning in every respect and patients in a geriatric ward. Assigning these two types of persons to the same category may not involve any conscious decision, but it is part of a complex cultural process which operates through the medium of language.[1] Language, which functions as a reality-constructing device, sets boundaries for our universe of imagery and associations and fuses concepts, myths and symbols into accepted forms of communi-cation. The various images of the 'old woman' in children's

13

literature exemplify this process: she may be a witch – associated with ugliness, infertility, wickedness, and demonic powers – or a grandmother or someone poor, frail, and degraded. These three different images, each internally complex, show how features of our culture are reflected in our personal perceptions of ageing. One of the aims of this book is to examine our society and our self-consciousness through the symbols and images involved in those perceptions.[2]

The allocation of space to the elderly (Rowles 1978) at once indicates their place in the community and instructs us as to the overall structure of society and the nature of social relationships prevailing within it. In biblical times, the 'elders', sages, wise men, and leaders, as guardians of the community, were allotted social and physical space at the gate of the town. Today their situation is just the opposite. From the almshouse and the workhouse through community-sponsored 'old-age homes' to the large denominational charities, institutional care for the aged implies marginality and isolation from the mainstream of society. Thus the allocation of territory becomes tantamount to social segregation. The old-age 'home' is in fact for people who have lost their homes. The use of this euphemism is telling, since such expressions generally indicate avoidance. The more recent term used to identify a territorial concentration of the elderly, 'geriatric centre', establishes the social fact that, as a result of shared medical problems, elderly people are assembled under the auspices of the branch of medical science that deals with ageing. This term reduces individuals to their impaired physiological aspects. Elderly people are no longer referred to in terms of social identities, rather it is the very absence of other imputed and acceptable identities that generates the concept of the old person as sick and in need of medical care.[3]

In the face of the contradictions, tensions, and ambiguities embedded in the concept of ageing, the gerontological literature is inadequate and inconsistent.[4] There are, of course, thematically coherent works; for example, Simone de Beauvoir's classic *The Coming of Age* (1975) argues that, in almost every society, the aged confront a disregard which gradually strips them of their status and rights. Other research, generally undertaken by American scholars, presents a more optimistic view, suggesting that ageing does not necessarily mean withdrawal, decline and depression but rather entails a reconstruction of life through personal revitalization and resocialization.

The massive pool of 'objective' data on ageing enables us to determine, for example, life expectancy which, in modern complex society, is in the range of seventy-five years for women and seventy-one years for men. This fact in itself is intriguing and raises questions about the division of labour within the family amongst the aged. Statistical investigation has also revealed a higher percentage of women than men in areas with high concentrations of aged people such as the inner city, day centres, and old-age homes (Hochschild 1973). Another noteworthy fact is the significant increase in the percentage of the aged in the overall population which has various implications for the perception of the aged on the part of the non-aged, the presence of the aged in different social settings, and their political-economic power. Knowledge of this kind is itself, however, the result of social interpretation. Tendentious presentation of information projects an ideologically inspired picture of ageing. The titles of gerontological books attest to their underlying assumptions: *Last Chapters* (Marshall 1980), *Readings in Aging and Death* (Zarit 1977), *Old and Alone* (Tunstall 1966), *The Ageless Self* (Kaufman 1986), *Number Our Days* (Myerhoff 1978a), *The Limbo People* (Hazan 1980a), *Older People and their Social World* (Rose and Peterson 1965), *The Last Frontier* (Fontana 1976), *Will You Still Need Me, Will You Still Feed Me When I Am 84?* (Francis 1984), *Growing Old: The Process of Disengagement* (Cumming and Henry 1961), *Old People – New Lives* (Keith 1982), *The Unexpected Community* (Hochschild 1973), *Idle Haven* (Johnson 1971), *Fun City* (Jacobs 1974).

There is a tendency, especially among those engaged in the provision of welfare services for the aged, to see them as a mass of material exigencies. The cataloguing of needs assumes that the researcher has access to and can correctly interpret the experience of being old, and this assumption may lead to the suggestion of strategies for 'successful ageing'. This concept, prevalent in the literature on the aged, implies not only the establishment of particular social services and the allocation of resources, but also the patronizing instruction of aged persons for better and fuller lives. Much of the research on ageing can be traced to particular economic and political interests.

15

One way of defining 'aged' is the seemingly unproblematic self-definition: an 'old person' is someone who regards him- or herself as such. In research conducted in an old-age home in which the average age of the residents was eighty-one years, however, 83 per cent were unwilling to see themselves as 'aged' (Coe 1965), and we have very little knowledge about the reasons for this. (The socio-cultural background of the respondents, the institutional setting, and the structure of the interview no doubt all contributed.)

Another definition of 'age' is socially constructed, composed of an infinite number of overlapping points of view with regard to a given person. Changing circumstances and the dynamics of social relationships make it difficult if not impossible to use such a definition rigorously. It is, however, possible to identify a number of attributes which suggest a broad social characterization of the concept.

A third definition with special appeal for academics is a scientific one: the 'aged' are those possessing a set of objectively determined properties that can be identified and measured. The most likely sources for such a definition are the life sciences: biology, bio-chemistry, genetics, and psychology. For us, however, the issue is the connection between any such scientific measure and the images of the aged generated in the course of human interaction. This connection will be neither direct nor deterministic since most scientific research is restricted in scope and confined to a limited scientific framework. Though useful within a particular research context, physiological measures are of limited use with respect to the emergence of the 'aged' as a social construct. The same is true of other 'objective' perspectives such as the focus on mental processes and personality changes characteristic of 'old age' (Birren and Schaie 1985).

The most prevalent of all definitions of 'aged' is the formal, bureaucratic one, also clearly socially constructed: an 'old person' is someone who has reached the age of sixty (if female) or sixty-five (if male).[5] Most of the social services and public resources assigned to the aged are based on such official arrangements. The impact of this bureaucratic definition on the fate of the elderly – determining their economic situation, their relationship to others, their self image – should not be underestimated.

Any theoretical perspective concerning ageing is replete with contradictions, conflicts, and paradoxes originating in our cultural system. These brief references to the terminology used in relation to the elderly serve to indicate that ageing is not a clear, coherently defined subject amenable to analysis in precise terms. In the following chapters it will further be argued that this state of confusion and inconsistency is reflected in the social world of the aged themselves and that the paradoxes inherent in the socio-cultural structure are paralleled in their self-realization. Though the 'aged' is a distinct symbolic category in our culture, the elderly, through their lived experience, are part and parcel of this culture. The articulation of the various components of cognition and behaviour in the aged self must, therefore, be regarded as mirroring the properties of the social order which the elderly inhabit and of which the construct of 'old age' is a significant constituent. Accordingly, the ensuing analysis will pursue the links between continuity and discontinuity, cultural diversity and human universals, meaning and control at both the macroscopic level of social structure and the microscopic level of the self. One arena in which these two levels meet is the identification of old people as a social problem.[6]

The social discourse on ageing involves a vocabulary that combines moral order and practical needs: 'handling', 'managing', 'organizing', 'looking after', 'caring for', 'placing' and 'planning'. Within it old age is seen as posing a threat to everyday conceptions of space, time, and meaning. Furthermore, the competition among various social agents, such as welfare workers, politicians and the clergy, over the ownership and representation of this assumed social problem transforms it into an issue deemed to belong to the public sphere, deserving of social attention and resources (Gusfield 1981). The most striking examples of this construction of ageing as a social problem are in the areas of health services, where the bulk of expenditure is allocated to the last years of life, and welfare policies that appropriate a proportion of national resources to care for the aged (see, e.g., Estes 1979; Phillipson 1982; Laslett 1989).

Manifestations of the 'problem' occur on two levels, the personal and the social. On the one personal level, our attitude to the aged is laden with guilt. Reinforced by the existential fear of ageing and its association with death, an apologetic, didactic, and value-oriented

17

ideology penetrates our consciousness and influences our behaviour. At the same time, economic interests and power considerations contradict it; competition in the labour market and pressure to control family assets are two examples of this type of constraint. On the social level, that of the determination of policies towards ageing, allocation of resources, planning of services, and the like, the aged person is conceived as dependent on the will of others. Whereas we often hear high-flown words about the need to enhance the participation of the elderly, to empower them, to allow them a voice in determining the organizational framework and administration of old-age homes, social clubs and day centres, the degree of involvement granted to the aged is generally restricted to particular spheres within a framework of dependency. The notion of the aged as a problem rests on the fundamental assumption that there is an unbridgeable gap between the 'aged' and 'society'. We tend to speak of the 'adaptation of the aged person to society', 'what society can do for the aged', and 'how the aged can "contribute" to society'. This distinction rests in turn on the assumption that the aged and the non-aged constitute two distinct categories of human beings. We speak as if we knew what society was (a sin of which this book is not exonerated). Though abstract, the system of images and concepts that we employ provides us with a sense of society as a concrete object, tangible and perceptible, with a real existence and integrity of its own. The aged are represented as an amorphous body distinct from and alien to society.

This barrier constitutes a separation not only on a horizontal dimension, that is, as a form of social segregation which defines the aged as non-humans and humans as non-aged, but also in time. Paradoxically, whereas the aged are seen as having long, rich, personal and social histories, we relate to them as discrete beings detached from their previous lives and from the social frameworks of the non-aged. Thus, the category of the aged not only remains unintegrated into society but also is sequestrated from it. This perception may then be used to legitimate homogeneous, segregated frameworks for the aged designed and administered by society at large. Some years ago, Age Concern, the British lobby, published a manifesto the opening statement of which was that as long as society related to the aged as a 'race apart' there would be no room for sensible discussion concerning the problems of the aged or their solutions. This statement is, however, self-contradictory, because defining the aged as a distinctive human group makes it impossible to comprehend their situation in terms of problems and solutions within the general human social framework.

The separation of the aged from society is manifest in a variety of ways and at a number of levels. The most telling instance is in the economic domain, in which the key assumption is that the aged are non-productive and that their contributions to and investments in society do not match the services and welfare they enjoy. These privileges can therefore be granted to the aged in return for their acquiescence in an economically marginal position. A lifetime of productivity is disregarded, and only the pecuniary present is taken into consideration. The aged are perceived as incapable of making any future returns, and any support rendered them is deemed a matter of charity and not a right. The anthropological literature attests that in many societies changes in the productive capacity of older persons do not necessarily entail the discontinuation of economic performance (Havighurst 1975; Kreps 1976; Schultz 1980; Espenshade and Braun 1983; Glascock and Feinman 1981). Rather, old people continue to contribute to the economy in other areas of social need in accordance with their abilities. In our society, such adjustments are rare. The fact that the aged are considered economically non-productive serves to legitimate their dependency. The question of productivity, however, is highly problematic. Although we are accustomed to measure investments and returns in terms of their monetary equivalents, the contribution of the aged cannot and need not be evaluated in this way. On the contrary, the unique productivity of the aged could and should be appraised in terms of its irreplaceability. The accumulated capital of a lifetime of human experience has no direct equivalent in the economic marketplace.

A further manifestation of the segregation imposed upon the aged is in the field of health services, where they receive intensive attention and care. Irrelevant to our discussion is the fact that many aged persons suffer from various illnesses; rather, it is ageing itself that is seen as a disease. The social image of the entire phenomenon of ageing has been transformed into a pathology. This perspective is

19

clearly exemplified in the social arrangement of an ordinary general hospital. Usually, hospital departments are organized in terms of type of illness or part of body and the medical functions that such departments provide. Three departments, however, are classified and defined in terms of the type of person treated in them: the children's, the maternity, and the geriatric. Although the people placed in the geriatric ward often suffer from a combination of serious diseases, it is not the functional description of these diseases that determines the assignment of patients to this particular ward. In other words, our society views ageing through the prism of illness. The aged have no social identity to speak of, and they lack clearly defined social roles. Thus they are seen as representatives of an abnormal social condition – in other words, unhealthy, even if from a strictly physiological point of view, they are well. From this perspective, bodily illness merely confirms or extends this social definition.

Any exception to the image of the elderly person as sick is perceived as enigmatic. This can be seen in the attitude towards persons who do not conform to this standard criterion of ageing as a pathology, for example, elderly persons who engage in sport (and may even surpass younger competitors, as may elderly marathon runners). Generally speaking, such people are viewed as freaks of nature; they become part of folklore. Indeed, many older persons may in fact make extensive and often shrewd use of these social expectations by adopting the 'sick' role. Anthropological research conducted amongst a group of institutionalized aged in France (Keith 1982) revealed that during the weekly visit with members of their families the aged would complain about being denigrated and depressed and about their meaningless lives. When the visit was over and their families had left, they would look around as if to say, 'Finally we can get back to normal life – we've given them what they wanted to see'. The commonly held image had been transformed into a tangible social fact.

The link between expected behaviour and language is manifest in the concept of 'adaptation' which pervades the gerontological literature (Pearlin and Schooler 1978; George 1979). On the surface, the concept appears scientific, objective, and neutral. In fact, however, it represents a world view which requires that the older person conform to the demands of society (see, e.g., Gubrium and Lynott 1983). To assess this adaptation, researchers usually ask older persons about their degree of 'life satisfaction'. Though it is doubtful whether one can meaningfully speak of general satisfaction, in the case of the aged it is considered appropriate to pose such questions and to expect reasonable and valid answers. In this context, 'life satisfaction' is mistaken for a scientific tool for measuring the degree of correspondence between the aged and society. In other words, it serves to widen the gap between what are perceived as two distinct human universes. Seemingly unequivocal answers to such questions may reflect no more than the elderly respondents' reluctance or inability to express their general 'life satisfaction' and/or perhaps, their desire to rid themselves of the irritating presence of the researcher, but they open the way for the planning of services for the aged. We tend to forget that the concept of adaptation itself is not only devoid of any scientific validity but also value-laden. Thus an apparently simple construct is at once inefficient and dangerous.

The concept of adaptation or adjustment is applied not only to the aged but to children, the sick, the handicapped, prisoners, rehabilitated offenders, the 'underprivileged', and immigrants. These are social categories for which the common denominator is dependency. Signs of adjustment on the part of these socially constructed human types imply surrender to social dictates, but through such compliance they may take their place in 'normal' society. For the aged, however, there is no hope of their re-entering society. For them 'adjustment' becomes complete acceptance of an irreversible change in the character of their lives.

The aged are conceived as a mass of needs bound together by the stigma of age. Stripped of their personalities and distinctive identities, first and foremost they are treated as old. Furthermore, since they are not identified with society, they become non-persons. In some societies, they are killed or abandoned (see de Beauvoir 1975: chapter 2); in others they are given the names or nicknames of animals (Hazan 1980b). Such manifestations of attitudes towards the aged as entities to be excluded from the realm of human beings are by no means confined to societies different from our own.

A more recent approach to the aged as a social problem views them as a deprived minority group (Streib 1965; Palmore and

Manton 1973) – an exploited sector capable of developing a sense of shared identity based on mutual interests and achieving common goals through collective action. Central to this approach is the notion that the aged themselves must determine their own social identity. It presupposes the possibility of transforming a negative social identity into a social asset. According to advocates of this position (see, e.g., Rose 1965; Hess and Markson 1980), a precondition for such a revolution in the status of the aged is the desire and determination on the part of the aged as a self-conscious group to change their destiny and to recognize their capacity to do so. Rudimentary movements of this kind have begun to emerge, but achievement of their objectives seems unlikely where the aged are denied all access to economic resources and political power. The importance of this approach in this context is that it too is framed in terms of the definition of the aged as a social problem.

The concrete problems commonly ascribed to older persons are in fact less important than the social definition projected and imposed upon them. Indeed, it could be said that the specific, concrete problems encountered by older people are the *result* of that definition. Non-aged persons who fall sick are never exclusively viewed as sick, and following recovery they are once again treated as healthy. Similarly, persons in dire economic straits are usually treated as capable of coping in the long term, and there are numerous social mechanisms whereby they may be returned to the fold. The situation of the aged, however, is radically different. In their case lack of adjustment is in fact 'adjustment'. To demonstrate that they are deserving of social support, they must display signs of such 'adjustment' that in any other social situation would be construed as abnormal. Conversely, those who speak their minds, ignore social criticism, and act in accordance with their own feelings are perceived as deviants in need of help.

It is clear from all this that the problem is not that of the aged themselves but of those who relate to them, and, similarly, that 'solutions' to the 'problem' do not address the aged at all but serve those for whom they are a burden. The different types of solutions to the 'problem' of ageing may be classified in terms of two primary axes, each of which represents a type of social relationship with the aged. The first axis consists of a continuum ranging from integration to segregation, from involvement to disengagement. At the integrationist end of the continuum, the proper attitude towards the aged is one of inclusion in multigenerational frameworks of various sorts; the aged are thought of as indistinguishable from the community. At the other end of the continuum, the segregationist, the aged are to be separated from social settings of which they were once a part. The second axis is the continuum between what might be termed humanization and dehumanization. At one end, the aged are viewed as complete human beings possessing coherent social identities and clearly defined social roles; at the other end, they are viewed as culturally ambiguous entities lacking some of the properties of human beings. Clearly no real-life social situation can manifest a fully humanistic perspective.[7] We never relate to others in terms of all their qualities. Other than in literary descriptions and philosophical discourse, no one can claim to interact with another person in an absolute and unmediated way. Rather, our relationships with others have various levels and multiple facets, personal and social. The argument here is that in the case of the aged, the multiple dimensions of what it is to be human are radically reduced and age itself becomes the predominant one.

The four combinations made possible by these two axes engender a multitude of contingencies. In the combination of integration and humanization, elderly people are both well integrated into their social environment and viewed as acceptable human beings. When integration is coupled with dehumanization, the aged live in the midst of society but are no longer regarded as ordinary human beings. The combination of segregation with humanization distances the elderly from the community of which they were once members but preserves their social identities. In the combination of separation and dehumanization the elderly are not only alienated but no longer regarded as human beings.

The combination of integration and humanization may be found in agricultural societies in which the elderly still control significant resources such as practical or ceremonial knowledge or land. A condition for their maintenance of control is the absence of literacy – the fact that they continue to provide orally transmitted information. In such cases, not only are they an integral part of society but they constitute an asset to be treated with respect and reverence. In the contemporary Western world examples of such societies are few and far between. There are, however, classes of elderly people who continue to enjoy positions of power. The best example of this is politicians, who, because they continue to have power, are never exclusively or even predominantly treated as old. Indeed, theirs is a source of authority that develops and becomes more sophisticated over time. Artists and intellectuals may also be included in this category.

The second configuration, the combination of integration and dehumanization, is best exemplified in the practice of forced retirement. In contemporary Western society, work is a central role; intimately associated with our deepest understanding of the value and virtues of a human being and the ethical justification of our very existence, it has significance for identity far beyond the economic sphere. Hence, when older people are forced to retire they confront serious problems of identity. The problem is exacerbated in the event that they continue to reside in the same setting. It is not surprising that discussion about the aged and their imputed problems often revolves around the question of pre-retirement programmes intended to ease the trauma of forced severance from the realm of work.

The third configuration, the combination of segregation and humanization, is illustrated by the new communities of the aged in the Western world, primarily in the United States (Byrne and Arden 1974; Heintz 1976; Jacobs 1975; Hochschild 1973; Keith 1980a, 1982) – self-administered, age-homogeneous collectivities in which they are able to function without disturbance in almost complete isolation from the outside world. (In some of these cases even family members are denied access without special permission.) Clearly, these communities require substantial financial resources and are generally inhabited by relatively well-off residents in areas where services can be obtained at reasonable cost. In some states, since community members create employment by consuming goods and services while at the same time making minimal use of state facilities, such social enterprises are viewed as a valuable resource and are actively promoted and encouraged (Heintz 1976). These communities, administered by the elderly themselves, can offer especially attractive conditions to their inhabitants, including services in particular demand by the elderly such as adequate medical facilities, nutritional attention and health care, recreational and leisure facilities, and, above all, security. It is worth noting that the success of such enterprises is not restricted to pre-planned communities for the wealthy. Similar success has been reported among communities that have emerged through force of circumstances (Hochschild 1973), as in the case of inner-city migration, where the local aged are the only residents to remain in the neighbourhood. Where a relatively poor population is marooned in this way the socio-cultural life of the aged demonstrates extraordinary vitality and creativity. The most intriguing interpretation of this success is that in communities of individuals with substantial resources the separation from the society at large remains incomplete. The wealthy are more likely to sustain an interest in their businesses and in the general economic life of the surrounding society which, in turn, sustains other familial and social ties. Since the separation is only partial, negative stereotypes may continue to penetrate into the community from the outside, thus inhibiting the residents' freedom for social creativity. In contrast, in communities with limited economic means the isolation is almost complete. The children, having left home and broken any economic ties, are not motivated to foster frequent communication with their parents. In order to make their day-to-day life more endurable, the elderly are forced to develop amongst themselves frameworks for mutual support and an active community life. In a situation of forced separation from the outside world, these individuals are given a fresh opportunity to develop and to flourish within, in spite of, or possibly because of their economic constraints.

The fourth configuration, separation and dehumanization, is perhaps the most familiar 'solution' to the 'problem' of the aged. In our society it is best exemplified by the old-age home. There is a wide variety of residential institutions for the aged, ranging from those designed for particular categories of the aged classified in terms of their level of mental and physical functioning, through those based on ethnic or professional commonalities, to those whose residents are heterogeneous and arbitrarily lumped together. Such institutions differ greatly in the availability of care facilities and services, in the collective profile of residents, in admission criteria, in living conditions and in socio-cultural environment. In some old-age homes, the treatment and provisions are below any acceptable minimum standard, sometimes to the extent of malnutrition, medical malpractice, and hazard to health. In effect these serve as almshouses for old people (Townsend 1962). Other homes, in exchange for substantial sums of money, offer services and facilities of the highest calibre.

The common denominator of all these institutions (with the possible exception of one type which will be described) is the unbridgeable gap between staff and inmates. The task of the former is to administer the daily lives of the latter, who are obliged to follow instructions and live under surveillance. The confrontation between staff and residents creates a social situation that is not exclusively characteristic of old-age homes but prevails in other social settings that sociologists call 'total institutions' (Goffman 1961), in which almost all of the day-to-day life of inmates is spent in the company of the same group of fellow inmates and under the control of one central authority. Examples of such institutions include prisons, ships at sea, military training camps, hospitals, boarding schools, and monasteries. In total institutions the authorities enforce rules and regulations not necessarily through any ill will (though this may sometimes appear to be the case) but as a result of the organizational imperatives of efficient administration. All such institutions are surrounded by social and physical boundaries by which the flow of information is controlled and internal indoctrination facilitated, thereby encouraging a high degree of dependency on the authorities on the part of the governed. The fact that the residents of old-age homes are elderly people adds a particular dimension to the socio-cultural systems created within them. For most residents the old-age home is not a transitory stage but the last stage in their lives, and the very existence of these institutions reflects the general social conception of the elderly as redundant, bothersome and disturbing. The implications of these two elements are that society allays its existential fears and relieves itself of guilt and daily nuisance by placing the old in a separate environment. The aged residents of such institutions are caught between three sources of identity: their past social relations with families, friends and colleagues, the institutional setting and an enforced new set of peers.

In some traditional societies, the configuration of segregation and dehumanization may take the form of the actual physical destruction of the elderly, usually with their consent. This 'solution' generally results from the fact that the aged person becomes an increasing economic burden. In societies of relative abundance dehumanization and separation may mean not only preserving the physical bodies of the aged but often sustaining them with elaborate medical care. (Calls for the physical elimination of the elderly were, however, made by some members of the 1960s counter-culture, who viewed the presence of old people as threatening the celebration of youth so characteristic of that time.)

It is indeed the presence of the aged in terms of their body-social versus their body-physical that is at the core of the cultural confusion from which the identification of 'problems' requiring 'solutions' arises. The language of separation, while sequestrating the aged from the rest of society, assigns significations about old age to their asocialized bodies. The body, with its material needs, somatic changes, and physiological functions, becomes the pivotal point for our relationship to old age. Having given the body a prominent role in the presentation of the social self (Goffman 1959; Stone 1970), our society has turned the ageing body into a carrier of collective stigma which falls short of the objectification and dehumanization sometimes termed 'social death' (Sudnow 1967; Kastenbaum 1977). The body is the hub not of cultural discourse (Lasch 1979; Foucault 1978; Turner 1984) but of its negation. Rather than generating meanings, even in the form of self-adulation, it is marginalized to the extent of symbolic invisibility (Gergen and Back 1966; Myerhoff 1978a). Meaning and control cease to inform each other.

In sum, we see that the two axes – segregation–integration, which is essentially social and organizational, and humanization–dehumanization, which is cultural and symbolic – provide a framework within which different images of ageing are formulated and disseminated and in the name of which the existential circumstances of the aged are determined.

2

The cultural trap: the language of images

The viability of stereotypes is often held to be inversely related to the amount of concrete evidence available about their objects: the more informed we are, the less valid is the stereotype. There is, however, considerable evidence that concrete information does not necessarily invalidate a stereotype but, on the contrary, may serve to reinforce it (Alport 1959). The information received about old people is often ambiguous, and because of this the stereotype overrides our perception of them even in face-to-face interaction. Stereotypes govern our behaviour by obscuring characteristics which, to an unbiased observer, would be clearly visible. A stereotype is presumed universally applicable, without regard to interpersonal differences. It is enormously flexible and therefore useful in handling variegated and changing situations; where it seems appropriate to shift attention to the concrete information at hand, a stereotype may be temporarily set aside. Stereotypes may display contradictions both internally and among themselves. All these characteristics of stereotypes are apparent in the attribution of cultural constructs to the aged.[1]

One of the most deeply rooted stereotypes of the aged is that they are conservative, inflexible, and resistant to change. The aged are perceived as incapable of creativity, of making progress, of starting afresh. Only in art and the domain of the spirit are they licensed to continue to be creative. 'Ordinary' old people are seen to have entered a state of intellectual sterility and emotional impotence.

Perhaps the most common manifestation of this general image of infertility and inertia is the perception of the aged as devoid of sexuality. Contrary to this popular perception, all the research evidence available categorically disproves the image of the elderly as asexual (Hendricks and Hendricks 1977). A further manifestation of this attitude is the imputation to the aged of inability to learn – to store and process information. Studies examining this hypothesis invariably demonstrate that, notwithstanding motoric and sensory deficiencies associated with the ageing process, there are no significant differences between older and younger people in their capacity to learn (Baltes and Schaie 1977). Indeed, when equal opportunities are granted to elderly students and personal motivation meets with social approval, they are capable of pursuing any course of study (Midwinter 1982, 1984). One of the arguments suggested by this line of research is that the apparent differences derive not so much from discrepancies in perception or in the ability to absorb and process new information as from different levels of technical skill, such as difficulties in hearing, sight, and coordination. Marked differences in modes of perception may also be attributed to gaps in formative life experiences having nothing to do with old age itself. Moreover, the social creativity of certain groups of older persons is often comparable with that of youth. The development of communities of the aged requires the organization of novel lifestyles and renewal of identity that would do justice to any young people's 'commune'. In terms of the cultural opportunities available for self-realization, life in these communities is often richer and more varied than that hitherto experienced by their inhabitants.

Another stereotype of old people is that they are 'senile'. Here there is an important difference between the formal medical definition and the image evoked by popular use of the term (Gubrium 1986). For the physician, senile dementia is a condition in which the blood vessels in the brain become clogged, reducing the supply of blood to the brain cells and leading to the death of those cells and the consequent loss of certain emotional and cognitive capacities. Another common form of brain pathology in the elderly, affecting approximately 10 per cent of old people, is the condition known as 'Alzheimer's disease', which causes changes in the brain tissue resulting in gradual loss of mental abilities such as memory, orientation, and verbal communication. Among lay people, there is a tendency to consider certain behaviour as evidence of senility, disregarding alternative explanations for that behaviour. The concept of senility, supported by the image of ageing as an illness, serves as an umbrella interpretation so wide that few old people can escape its range. Furthermore, since one of the presumed consequences of senility is inability to make decisions, it is often used to justify the assumption of responsibility by others for older people's lives. Thus the aged may be committed to institutional custody against their will on the grounds that they are incapable of handling their own affairs. This move often entails the exertion of socio-psychological pressure on older persons to act in accordance with the objects of those who take charge of their interests. The attribution of 'senility' to the aged may serve as a powerful weapon in the hands of those who seek to deprive them of control of and sometimes to appropriate their property, capital, and other material assets. The fact that few offenders are charged with criminal activity in cases of this kind suggests a conspiracy of silence that benefits from the fear and dependency of the elderly victims.

Failure to distinguish genuine physiological senility from imputed social senility reinforces the notion that gradual biological deterioration (resulting in mental erosion) is inevitable, uncontrollable, and irreversible. Observations conducted in day centres for the elderly have revealed, in contrast, that some who had been regarded as senile prior to their admission showed signs of resumed mental alertness (Hazan 1980a). These elderly persons may not have been physiologically senile; rather, their behaviour may have been a response to their socio-cultural situation.

The mirror image of this stereotype is the idea that old people are supernaturally wise, that is to say, possessed of a perspective on reality of an entirely different order to that of ordinary persons. On occasion we ask their advice, attempting to draw on their life experiences for answers to our most fundamental existential questions. In some societies, such reverence is traditionally bestowed on the seer and the wise man; in others, a parallel may be found with the madman and the court jester, ambiguous symbolic types[2] of a similar stereotypical configuration. Clearly, persons who are supposed to be incapable of making decisions in day-to-day life cannot be expected to offer reliable guidance. The attribution of the latter capacity to the elderly is made possible by the image of them as preoccupied with matters of the spirit. In fact, however, research demonstrates that old people just as often abandon the path of religion, reject life-long metaphysical world views, and adopt cynical and secular viewpoints (Myerhoff 1978a: chapter 2). This process of disenchantment is often construed as 'withdrawal', 'regression', or 'stubbornness' – all terms indicating non-compliance and resistance to social expectations.

Since the elderly are conceived of as incapable of initiative and sound judgement as to their own needs, frameworks for their management are designed by others that impel them into dependence. Old people who enter old-age homes as independent individuals are immediately denied their freedom, and it may come as no surprise that they soon demonstrate signs of withdrawal and indifference.

Alongside and contradictory to this image of powerlessness and dependence, older people are often seen as disturbing and threatening. It is much more difficult, for example, to recruit staff for services relating to the aged, in particular services entailing physical contact, than for work of a similar nature with children or the handicapped. Similarly, geriatrics suffer from a severe shortage of qualified manpower. While there are no doubt a number of reasons for this shortage, one of them is fear of, and resistance to becoming professionally and emotionally involved with old people (Hochschild 1983). This revulsion arises from the connection between the old and death (which, with increasing life expectancy, has gained empirical validity in the course of the past century), the image of infertility and asexuality associated with them and our disgust with human excrement and other bodily discharges. Incontinence, from drooling to involuntary defecation, is a reminder of the association between old age and corporeal disintegration.[3] Thus the aged are conceived of as at once dependent, incapable of influencing or controlling their environments, and threatening. In traditional societies, older people are often victims of witchcraft accusations. This indictment, the cultural manifestation of marginality and powerlessness, may lead to trial by poison ordeal, excommunication, banishment, and death (Turnbull 1984: 231–8).

Another stereotype is that the aged dwell on and draw their life meaning from the past. The present is deemed to hold no real interest for them, and we are often told that in order to understand and communicate with them it is imperative to appeal to their nostalgic recollections. In diametric opposition to this, it is often held that little interests them but the immediate gratification of their most basic day-to-day needs. When we wish to ignore those needs, it is convenient to say that the aged live in the past. When we want to dismiss their past status, it is convenient to argue that they live for the present.

This flexibility in stereotypic thinking is pertinent to yet another stereotype of old people – that they seek the company of their peers for reasons of pure sociability rather than from any desire for practical, instrumental gain or as part of a quest for meaning, identity and knowledge. According to this stereotype, the elderly are presumed to socialize with other persons as a panacea for all psychological and social maladies. The practical implementation of this stereotype is the allocation of significant amounts of social and economic resources to the establishment of old-age clubs and day centres in order that the aged may huddle together to enjoy the remedial benefit of each other's company. In contradiction to this imputed desire for company for company's sake, aged people may also be viewed as willingly detaching themselves from society, content with their own company or that of their nearest and dearest. In this view, elderly persons have strong ties to their immediate social mileux, and it is necessary to develop community services to enable them to maintain their familiar networks. Yet another contradictory stereotype is that the aged are prisoners of space and time, existential loners doomed to solitude and withdrawal. This view provides tacit justification for removing them from their social settings and relocating them in care facilities.

Finally, perhaps the most extreme and omnipresent stereotype of the aged is that they are depressed, unhappy, and pervaded with a sense of failure, disintegration, and pointlessness. It would be easy to refute the alleged universality of this and all other stereotypes, but the point here is that stereotypes are useful for camouflaging the social arrangements which we impose upon the aged members of our society. As the unspoken assumptions upon which 'scientific' theories of ageing are constructed, they become doubly dangerous, being mindfully or inadvertently employed to determine the fate of fellow human beings.

3

The personal trap: the language of self-presentation

If we accept that aged people are surrounded by a society that assigns them false images and that they are therefore trapped in a labyrinth of distorting mirrors, then the question arises of what self-conception they can possibly project.[1] According to the concept of the 'looking glass self' (Mead 1934; Cooley 1972) we see ourselves as we imagine others see us, and therefore the behaviour of older people and their attitudes towards themselves are shaped and reinforced by society's prevailing images of them. By adopting these images, the elderly in turn confirm and strengthen them.

Old people, for example, are thought to dress in drab, uniform clothing appropriate to the dull world in which they are considered to live. Many elderly people, upon accepting the label of 'aged', do indeed change their style of dress. Those who are reluctant to alter their appearance or prefer the fashionable arouse derision or surprise. A more extreme example is the physical limitations which older people adopt once they accept their definition as aged. Some may begin to stoop and shuffle, others may develop hearing deficiencies that have no apparent physiological basis (a kind of 'social deafness' that develops when people consciously or unconsciously choose not to hear). Some complain of deteriorating vision, others adopt movements characteristic of the physically handicapped in the absence of any such serious limitations (Esberger 1978; Levy 1979). Many older persons seek what they now regard as appropriate forms of social activity; they join old-age clubs and day centres or the 'club house of the park benches', where they engage in seemingly aimless conversations. All these types of behaviour bolster the image of the aged as needy, hopeless, sick, and incapable of social involvement – in short, people whose lives are no longer worth living.

In order to be acceptable to others, the elderly may make an effort to appear harmless, inoffensive, and easy-going. Some may go farther, attempting to efface their sexual identities. Fully capable of engaging in sexual activity from a biological point of view, they behave as if they had lost all erotic desire. Again, older people are often resistant to learning, adopting society's assumption that they are incapable of absorbing and acquiring new knowledge.

What we have here is apparently a vicious circle wherein the behaviour adopted by the elderly reinforces the negative images attached to them. However, a closer look at this psychological model of internalization reveals that it may be challenged on three counts. First, in line with the sociological concept of anomie – the absence of social values and norms – it may be argued that the sense of alienation experienced by old people is so strong that conventional social pressures operate to a far lesser degree than they do under ordinary circumstances. According to this view, the aged enjoy relative freedom. Because of the relaxation of social control and the disarray and lack of coordination of the various elements making up their social milieux, the aged are relatively free to manoeuvre and recognize the scant resources at their disposal to suit their needs. Second, the aged have personal histories and present commitments, involvements, and social networks that cannot be dismissed out of hand. Finally, the situations of elderly persons undergo transformations which offer them the opportunity to exercise a certain degree of freedom of choice. In sum, the impression that older people are trapped by the social images applied to them is often incorrect. In fact they employ a variety of behavioural strategies to counter those images.

One such strategy, rooted in a discrepancy between behaviour and conviction, is a mechanical and ritualized conformity to social expectations in selected settings – for example, in the presence of strangers. Among their peers, in contrast, these individuals may be able to explore newly acquired rewarding self-images and social identities in the company of others subject to similar pressures (Keith 1980a).

34

Another behavioural response is withdrawal – rejection of society's expectations through dissociation from them. Detachment from the surrounding society is achieved through immersion in recollections and reminiscences. This behaviour is prevalent among significant numbers of the elderly, especially in old age homes or other environments which exert strong and ongoing pressures on the aged (Vesperi 1980).

Yet another reaction may be described as rebellion – the dismissal of the basic cultural assumptions upon which the stereotypes of the aged are constructed – and may take two different forms. The first is defiance, and elderly persons adopting this approach may be characterized as 'stubborn' or 'contrary'. Examples of such acts of rebellion include appearing in public places or in institutional settings dressed in a sloppy or indecent fashion, stockpiling food, or engaging in petty theft. By perpetrating minor offenses they declare their independence and force others to pay attention. In effect, this behaviour is a plea for social recognition of selfhood, dignity, and the right to free expression. Actions with no apparent rational explanation that are commonly ascribed to senility are made explicable in this light. A constructive form of rebellion involves intentional separation from the oppressive milieu of everyday life in order to construct an alternative reality. On occasion this phenomenon is accompanied by the development of an ideology, sometimes to the point of constituting a 'counter-culture' of the aged. Provided that the separation is well defined and the barriers and boundaries firm, aged persons may thus create amongst themselves an alternative social world.

A further response on the part of the aged may be described as 'walking a tightrope'. This strategy implies taking a great deal of care not to stumble into the social traps laid for the elderly by selecting the symbols, situations, and the people over which they have control and rejecting the rest. The aged may move, for example, to settings inhabited primarily by old people and detached from family frameworks, discard the symbols and insignia of their former social status, and cease to speak in terms of change or future social rewards.

Sometimes symbols of weakness, dependency, and impotence may be transformed into signs of strength, activity, and integrity.

For example, the political movement in the United States called the Grey Panthers (a label adopted from the Black Panthers, a group which converted the social stigma of colour into a source of pride) seeks to transform the position of the elderly from feebleness to power sharing in the making of policy. The movement has in fact succeeded far beyond expectations – it has been instrumental in changing a number of age-discriminating laws and altering the atitude towards the aged in a variety of sectors of American society. This success is due not only to its effective mobilization of sympathy but, in large part, to the focused and efficient recruitment of political and economic resources at the disposal of a substantial portion of elderly American citizens (Jacobs and Hess 1978).

An alternative response on the part of old people consists of deciding for themselves to retire from their earlier occupations and pursue new directions. Such a change relatively late in life is possible in our society because life expectancy continues to rise and physical afflictions are on the decline. In some cases, retirement may take place as early as fifty-five, leaving a significant number of active years between retirement and death. This gap may often be as much as twenty or thirty years – enough time to start afresh. Such phenomena, however, remain rare though there is some evidence for late career changes, particularly in business and the arts.

Given sufficient means, the elderly person can travel and explore new horizons. Many older people feel suddenly free to engage in often harsh social criticism, daring to say what others cannot because they are no longer subject to the normal social pressures. In essence, the social vacuum in which they find themselves gives them license to act as if they had nothing to lose, an attitude reinforced by the tendency to humour the aged. In this they may be compared to the court jester who can say anything that occurs to him without fear of penalty (see Handelman 1981). Only marginal social types can afford to indulge in social behaviour otherwise illegitimate. (Perhaps, indeed, it is their marginality that is the source of the wisdom sometimes attributed to the elderly.)

Finally, perhaps the most extreme reaction to the identity crisis of the aged is self-inflicted death, whether by suicide or euthanasia. The will to die, be it conscious or unconscious, is a significant factor in determining 'the hour of our death' (Ariès 1983); conversely, the anticipation of an important occasion such as a birthday or the arrival of a loved one may prolong life (Zarit 1977: 282). Anthropologists are familiar with ritualistically inflicted forms of voodoo death, whereby the community declares a person socially dead and that person often dies without any trace of a biological cause. It may be that forces of a similar biopsychocultural nature are at work in our own society.[2]

ETHNOGRAPHIC REFLECTION: PRACTICES OF SEPARATION

The transition from a multidimensional existence to membership in a one-dimensional category may be understood in empirical terms of symbolic labelling and social relocation. The following case study, based on anthropological research in an old-age home, illustrates these two interwoven processes.

The old-age home in question was administered by Mishaan, a welfare organization affiliated with the largest trade union federation in Israel, the Histadrut. Eligibility for Mishaan services was dependent upon being a member (or the parent of a member) of the Histadrut. Such membership, however, was by no means a sufficient condition for admission. The imbalance between the limited number of vacancies in the old-age home and the growing demand for them made selection in favour of the able-bodied inevitable. In addition to being able-bodied and mentally alert, to enter the home and stay there required the aged to use personal contacts and wield political power within the organization.

Once admitted, inmates themselves were primarily responsible for whether they were judged fit to remain. In the terminology of the home they were under threat of removal should they become incapable of 'proper functioning', that is looking after themselves. Although certain vague criteria guided this assessment, it was open to various interpretations, and lack of functioning might range from mobility difficulties to incontinence and mental disturbance. 'Functioning' also included participation in the social life of the home. Active involvement in group activities and public meetings was highly praised by the director, who lost no opportunity to stress the direct link between social involvement and 'proper functioning'.

Removal from the home was perceived as the start of an

inevitable process of deterioration ending in death. For most inmates, death seemed close both cognitively and physically. Transfer to the sickrooms served as a kind of preparation for the onset of death, since in many instances inmates never returned to their rooms. Other inmates tended to avoid the sick wing. It was customary not to talk about the death of an inmate; in the event that a death was mentioned, it was emphasized that life goes on despite it. This denial of death was even more striking in the inmates' perception of the structure of the old-age home. At the top of the ladder were the active and healthy in mind and body, while at the bottom were the physically and mentally frail. Ironically, it was the latter category that constituted the physical and cognitive barrier between the former and death. The perceived gulf between them was expressed in the derogatory labels attached to the frailer inmates (the 'exhibition', 'vegetables', 'animals'), which served to exclude those so designated from any human frame of reference. Since the frailer inmates were the most likely candidates for transfer and for death, the creation of this non-human category served as a barrier both against death and against the possibility of removal from the home. Thus, a sort of social death sentence had been imposed upon them.

4

The theoretical trap: the missing language

The quest for the universal in research on ageing can be divided into four phases. The first, which might be termed the 'functional approach', consisted of the cross-cultural examination of the division of labour and the allocation of resources in society, and it revealed that the status of the aged was largely determined by their mastery of socially valued assets and functions. Pioneered by Simmons (1945), it was based on an extensive ethnographic survey of the role of the aged in seventy-one pre-industrial societies. This functional orientation was elaborated and extended by scholars such as Maxwell and Silverman (1970), who focused on the importance of information and knowledge as a social resource, and Glascock and Feinman (1981), who examined the asset value assigned to the elderly.

A more interactional view of the response of the elderly to their existential conditions, the 'adaptive' approach, took an uncompromising stand on the question of the accommodation between the elderly and society. A concept of 'successful ageing' involved the relation between personal adjustment to impending death and the imputed interests of the overall social system (Cumming and Henry 1961). Clark and Anderson's (1967) study of the nexus between personality configurations and cultural patterns in American society distinguished five adaptive modes on the part of the aged. Classifications of adaptive responses based on compatibility between cultural opportunities and personal traits were further developed by other scholars (Smith-Blau 1973; Fontana 1976).

A third phase, combining elements of 'functional' and 'adaptive' approaches, proposed a dynamic structural explanation of the links between socio-cultural processes and responses to old age on the part of elderly individuals and groups. Cowgill and Holmes (1972) traced the effects of modernization and industrialization on attitudes towards the aged in eighteen societies, while Goody (1976) examined the implications of the domestic unit as a system of production and reproduction on the status of the old in pre-literate societies. Another structural approach was the investigation of age as a stratifying force in society.

A fourth phase, responding to the emphasis on social transitions in the interpretation of ageing, attributed psychological constants to the construction of identity in old age. It was assumed that the sense of personal continuity furnished by culture would sustain the ageing self throughout its vicissitudes (Myerhoff and Simic 1978; Kaufman 1986).

Common to all these phases was the pursuit of an acontextual common denominator of ageing despite the obvious immense diversity of later life (see Amoss and Harrell 1981a). To get to grips with the 'phenomenon of ageing' the student, although probably convinced that the old should be treated first and foremost as individual human beings, was compelled to justify his research by representing ageing as a single socio-cultural configuration governed by its own rules. This frame of reference assumes an identification of ageing with its representatives that does not withstand scrutiny. Just as racial stereotypes are not to be mistaken for the real attributes of the people to whom they refer, so the cultural concept of ageing must not be confused with the actual existential experience of being old. Further, if ageing is to some extent unique, then the social scientists, unless they are themselves aged, are robbed of their main tool – the capacity to share the experience of the subjects of study – and forced to fall back on theories and concepts drawn from other fields of research.

One such concept – role (see Atchley 1977; George 1980) – is borrowed from the theatre. The theatrical performance as an analogy to society implies a world in which the script consists of social norms, the audience consists of the persons to whom the actors relate in playing given roles and whose cheers or jeers place constraints on the performance, and a move backstage allows for a change of roles. In short, the unity of plot, space, and time inherent in a theatrical performance serves as a convenient model for the pursuit of consistency, meaning, and a sense of continuity in social reality.

A central role is membership in the family unit (see Townsend 1957; Hareven 1978; Brubaker 1983; Bengtson 1979; Wenger 1984). For the aged, however, the role of family member is inherently ambivalent. On the one hand, they are responsible for the very existence of their families; on the other, they confront centrifugal forces separating them from them. The sociologist must construct a conception of the aged's family role that accommodates the emergent discrepancy between their symbolic representation of the family and their actual position as a redundant and sometimes burdensome part of it.

Old age robs the parental role of its essence by undermining the traditional hierarchical relationships of authority. Moreover, role reversal may occur with regard to the relations between man and wife. The disengagement which the aged male experiences in his family relations is far stronger and more dramatic than the corresponding experience of the woman. This difference derives both from society's sex-related division of labour and from the difference in life expectancy between the two categories (see Atchley and Miller 1983; Dougherty 1978; Lopata 1983; Matthews 1979). In a society in which the male is the primary breadwinner and the woman responsible for the domestic realm, the discontinuity experienced by the older woman is not so sharp, since she is not compelled to relinquish a lifetime of employment and her continuing role as wife provides her with a link to the social network cultivated in the course of her life. The man, in contrast, is cut off from his workmates on retirement, and from their shared interests and social world (see Altergott 1988; Morris and Bass 1988; Graehner 1980). Since their life expectancy is much greater, however, many more women find themselves alone in old age, sometimes having to look after their own widowed mothers. Indeed, many of the spontaneously emergent age-homogeneous communities consist in the main of elderly widows.

The difficulty in applying sociological definitions of family roles to aged people is that these definitions were created for persons in the thirty- to fifty-year age group. The parental custodial role, for example, usually lasts for approximately twenty years, and it is inappropriate to apply the criteria of guardianship, parental, financial responsibility, and socialization to persons no longer caught up in such obligations. A similar situation exists in relation to work roles, which, in our society, are of enormous significance in terms of self-image, sense of place in the world, and social interaction and identity. Upon retirement, the work role dissipates or changes, and the aged face the loss of former sources of power, respect, opportunities for advancement, and social rewards. What might be called political roles are social positions by which the aged continue to influence others (Werner 1981; Guillemard 1983; Riley 1979). One kind of power is tied to the social resources of employment, and with retirement this power is greatly reduced. Another is based on economic resources independent of the labour market. It is often interwoven into the mastery of organizational structures and can be neither acquired nor terminated through formal procedures; hence the ability of some leaders to maintain and even reinforce their roles beyond official retirement.

With this single exception, the change in the lives of the aged renders the concept of role inappropriate as a focus for the analysis, description, and understanding of their world. Old age is an increasingly dependent state, and the disintegration of the peer group and the shared negative self-image of those remaining make it increasingly difficult for aged persons to benefit from a sense of belonging and endow themselves with a positive identity. A number of 'roles' have nevertheless been proposed for the aged, but none of them really qualifies as such.

The 'role' of retiree or pensioner is the polar opposite of the work role and primarily consists of the mastery of leisure (though leisure, in the sense of the opposite of work, does not exist for the aged). The aged's task in life is to fill vacant time with hobbies and other activities that others deem fit for them. They are placed in 'occupational therapy' groups and encouraged to engage in handicrafts such as basket weaving, embroidery, knitting, and sewing – activities that are often not only foreign to them but are perceived as demeaning.

Another 'role' often attributed to old people is grandparent (see

Cunningham-Burley 1987; Bengtson and Robertson 1985), and it too is rife with paradox. On the one hand, we expect grandparents to demonstrate tremendous emotional involvement in their grand-children and to provide unlimited services and assistance. On the other hand, their involvement in decision making about the fate of these offspring is extremely limited. The 'role' entails reciprocal relations only with the grandchildren, who, structurally speaking, occupy a similar social position: they too are dependent, considered incapable of engaging in relationships beyond their peers, and socially marginal. In a sense, neither human category belongs to the 'real world' (on attitudes towards children, see Sheleff 1981). As a result of a high degree of occupational mobility, adults in the United States seldom live near their parents, and therefore it is impossible for the elderly to remain in constant touch with their grandchildren and to express their presumed 'grandparental drive' in the socially prescribed fashion. Consequently, we find older people adopting 'grandchildren' who are not their biological offspring but the wards of social workers or probation officers, supposedly to acquire an outlet for their ascribed emotional need to give affection to others. 'Pet therapy' in the treatment of psychological distress amongst the aged is yet another example of the social recognition of the scarcity of roles that characterizes this stage of the life cycle. The pet is supposed to provide unconditional loyalty and affection, thereby replacing no longer available human bonding (see, e.g., Savishinsky 1985). Underlying these forms of attachment is the assumption that the 'role' of grandparent is natural to the aged and must therefore be encouraged. Research indicates, however, that this is not neces-sarily the case and that in fact much apparently 'grandparental' behaviour is misconstrued as such. In fact, old people are often simply interested in maintaining connections with their children through the least contentious channel, perhaps reestablishing pre-viously tenuous links (Clavan 1978). Furthermore, in many instances, grandparents are geographically distanced from their families either because they are committed to an alternative way of life or because geographic distance imposes upon them the adop-tion of alternative everyday relationships.

Yet another 'role' often projected onto older people is that of patient. I have argued that the pathology of the body is transformed into social pathology that finds its symbolic expression in the attribution of diseases and physical malfunctioning to old people. It is indisputable that many elderly people are afflicted with chronic as well as acute illnesses – a fact that gives apparent corroboration to the association between being old and being sick. Moreover, the fact that aged people often fall victim to a number of illnesses simultaneously serves to defeat any attempt to escape the trap of self-evident pathology. From the elderly's point of view, acceptance of the sick 'role' is one of the easiest ways to gain secondary social rewards – attention and consideration – that would not otherwise be obtained. The 'role' of patient separates the aged from their environments, since illness is construed as a temporary or permanent suspension of other social roles and identities (Rosow 1974).

One further 'role' attributed to the aged is volunteer. Involvement in the affairs of the community is seen to substitute for eroded social status and provide a semblance of integration and inclusion. According to the volunteer model, good deeds are their own reward, and it is considered entirely legitimate to offer a reward of this nature to older people. Devoid of social status, prestige, and financial remuneration, voluntarism in old age offers the privilege of 'contribution' to society as its main return. This mock inclusion in society is even more evident in yet another pseudo-role generally assigned to those forced to leave high-status positions in politics or business. Endowed with formal tokens of authority, respect, and honour, this 'role' bears the ceremonial title of adviser, president, governor, or lord. Powerless to influence decision-making processes, the incumbents of this role are living symbols of past glory, present values, and future aspirations.

All these 'roles' have well-defined limits. The aged are prohibited from interfering, making decisions, expecting any reward, or engaging in reciprocal relationships. These specially created 'roles' support and reinforce prevailing social conditions of segregation, ambiguity, and alienation. Furthermore, they serve as a means of social control, protecting other sectors of society from the intervention of the aged. Lacking any positive content, they convey to the aged the message that they are at best marginal and at worst redundant.

If the concept of role is inapplicable to ageing, then a counter-construct is required. One candidate is the *non sequitor* 'roleless role' (Burgess 1950). Other concepts in the same spirit of negation include 'role exit' (Smith-Blau 1973), 'no exit' (Marshall 1979), or 'deculturalization' (Anderson 1972), all of which assume that the aged, having lost their social and cultural identity, may no longer be described in terms of positive cultural symbols. In spite of this difficulty, many sociologists have advanced general theories of ageing, suggesting causal linkages between conceptual postulates and empirical evidence to explain why human beings behave as they do. One of the principal challenges confronting any theoretical explanation is to encompass the totality of the subject. Ageing has biological, psychological and sociological aspects, and the challenge of describing the relationships among them remains unmet because the issue has been addressed in terms of the vocabulary of 'roles' and 'identities' rather than within the framework of meaning and control. Furthermore, the effects of viewing ageing as a social problem permeate a great many social-scientific perspectives. In a fundamental departure from scientific practice, terms such as 'adjustment' and 'maladjustment' are employed as measurable, analytically valid parameters for evaluating and understanding old people's lives.

One cluster of theories addresses the social status of the aged by identifying the forces that shape it. One of the most intriguing of these is disengagement theory (Cumming and Henry 1961). When the theory was first advanced it made ripples in the sociological world by challenging common social perceptions of the aged (see, e.g., Maddox 1964; Henry 1964; Kalish 1972; Hochschild 1975; Gordon 1975; Cumming and Henry 1976; Sill 1980). It defied the conventional notion that the apparently universal marginality of the aged is the result of pressures on them and contrary to their desires by proposing that successful ageing is contingent upon the mutual disengagement of the aged and their social environment. According to the theory, disengagement takes place on three levels. On the general societal level, the presence of the aged is redundant and disturbing. The social system is impeded in its operation by the presence of elements whose sudden and final departure from it might cause dramatic disruption. In these circumstances, social forces pre-empt the rupture by expelling the elderly from the social

45

world. This argument, founded on the assumed 'benefits' and 'needs' of the society, assumes tacit consensus as to the essence of the social good, which must override individual needs. It also views the aged and society as separable entities. On the second, behavioural level, disengagement strikes the desired balance between expectations and ability. As the aged's control of their environment diminishes, expectations of them must be adjusted. Mutual disengagement allows for the reorganization of resources to meet personal needs and social imperatives.

On the third level, disengagement allows the aged to prepare for death. As social roles gradually dissolve and sources of energy dwindle, older persons invest all their remaining strength in efforts to smooth the path towards their inevitable demise. Detachment proceeds from the outer circles of social involvement, such as employment, community, and neighbours, through friends and family, and the force that motivates and regulates it is inherent in the individual.

This theory is built upon a number of far-reaching, thought-provoking assumptions which are, by definition, not amenable to validation or refutation. They form a self-fulfilling logical structure within which empirical evidence is examined and conclusions reached. The system can, however, be challenged on a number of levels. First, the claim to the universality of the process of disengagement requires ample and unequivocal cross-cultural proof, and in fact evidence gathered in different cultures by social anthropologists lends it no support (see, e.g., Talmon-Garber 1962). Second, the assumption that disengagement is inevitable leads to a view of all behaviour as 'desirable' or 'undesirable' according to the degree of disengagement manifested. Any struggle against disengagement is regarded as doomed to failure because it opposes socio-psychological law. The sociological origins of disengagement theory lie not in empirical research on ageing but in an approach that dominated the social sciences from the beginning of the century and reached its zenith in American sociology during the 1950s. This perspective, known as functionalism, was based on an analogy between human society and the biological organism. Society was viewed as a body containing a system of mutually interdependent organs, each of which had its own particular function. The social body was said to be born, live, wither, and die like any other organism. Accordingly, disengagement theory assumes that society has needs which the older person must accommodate in order not to upset its proper functioning.

At first glance, disengagement theory appears innocuous, but when it is adopted by planners of social services and those who deal with the aged it may cause great harm. It makes it easy to argue that the aged actually desire segregation, and hence to withhold social services from them. Thus, it may be used to justify reduction of the resources allocated to the aged and planning of services without consulting those for whom they are intended. Stripped of its universalistic and deterministic character, however, it may be used to investigate a variety of forms of voluntary disengagement which may be strategies appropriate to particular existential conditions. Strategic choices may even include re-engagement, and the latter is in fact the focus of an alternative approach, the activity perspective.

The activity approach was developed in the United States during the late 1950s and early 1960s (see Havighurst 1954, 1963; Havighurst et al. 1964; Orbach 1973; Kalish and Knudtson 1976). Lacking any internal theoretical consistency, it argues that a satisfactory life requires investment of energy in socially sustained self-fulfilment and maintenance of involvement in groups, roles, and activity circles of all sorts. Proponents of one version of this approach argue that the aged must attempt to preserve continuity with their lives (see Myerhoff and Simic 1978 for references). Meaningful activities cherished and enjoyed during the course of life must be maintained, albeit in modified form, throughout old age. A second version argues that since former life activities cannot be maintained into old age, the aged should find alternative ways of engaging in creative social activity, particularly among their peers. This notion of activity at all costs reflects a paramount value of American society, whose members seek to justify their existence through constant social involvement.

Generally speaking, comparison of the activity and disengagement perspectives reveals two complementary aspects of contemporary Western society. On the one hand, once people cease to be 'productive' and to 'contribute' to society, they are expected to be put out to graze. On the other hand, they are expected to maintain a constant quest for a sense of achievement. Apparently these contradictory models of behaviour, placed within a cultural context, constitute dimensions of the 'American dream', which espouses the unlimited right to individual self-realization and the priority of the social order over individual needs.

Other, more recent perspectives view the status of the aged person as determined by natural rather than social forces. Such socio-biological theories assume an inherent tendency of human-kind to preserve its genes. They argue that human beings conduct their social lives with the implicit goal of maintaining their own biological continuity and that of the human species at large (Wilson 1975). The challenge posed by the aged as biologically defunct (Berry 1981) is met by the proposal that the aged are vital in main-taining cultural continuity, which, in turn, contributes to the pre-servation of the overall gene pool. Thus, the evolutionary role of the no longer fertile human female is care giver to her son's off-spring, who carry and thereby preserve her genes (Katz 1978). In this view, the aged are guardians of culture, which is also subject to the law of the preservation of the species. Socio-biological theories do not explain specific phenomena, and they provide a perspective on reality which does not seem to lend itself to empirical testing.

Another theoretical approach focuses on the structure of the aged's social relationships rather than their social status. This approach, informed by exchange theory (Dowd 1975; Bengtson and Dowd 1980), suggests that human beings expect to receive something in exchange for any investment in social relations and thus a system of cost–benefit mutuality and interpersonal reinforcement is generated. Exchange theory argues that the situ-ation of the aged in society must be seen over time and that an assumption concerning the time frame of investment and return must be added to the proposition to render it workable. Rewards are not immediate, and individuals' investments during the course of their lives entitle them to reap the benefits in old age. There is very little empirical evidence to support this idealized picture of lifelong, cohesive inter-generational relations.[1] In general, in the absence of formal guarantees such as insurance arrangements and state welfare services, the notion of balanced exchange over time seems inconsistent with the prevalence of dependency and powerlessness among the aged and the limited resources available to them.

The theory of exchange offers understanding neither of the meanings assigned to investments of different sorts nor of the different costs of such investments. In a particular society, for instance, a certain object may be thought of as valuable by virtue of its rarity, and the reward for such an investment may be very high. In another society or under different circumstances, that commodity may acquire a different value. The care given to offspring, for example, may lose its value with the disintegration of the social system. Further, ongoing exchange relationships involve a conception of the passage of time between investment and return, but among the elderly time is not measured in the same intervals as it is among the career-oriented non-aged.

A final theoretical approach, conventionally labelled 'symbolic interaction', attempts to consider the meanings attached to social action. It is based on the assumption that interaction is a negotiated trade of meaning-laden units or symbols. Symbolic interactionism focuses on the shared symbols and meanings by which reality is constructed. According to this perspective, a system of cultural communication assumes that (1), despite the ambiguity of symbols and concepts, shared understanding can be established among members of the same cultural unit, and (2) that socialization moulds world views in line with a symbolic heritage.

The situation of the aged in contemporary society gives the lie to both these assumptions. The separation between 'the aged' and 'society', and 'deculturation' which strips the old of their social endorsements undermines the edifice of shared meanings that makes mutual understanding possible, even among the aged themselves. This situation is further aggravated in modern or postmodern society, in which traditional images are subject to fragmentation and transformation.

Notwithstanding the considerable differences among these theoretical models, all of them suggest that old age is subject to the unmediated impact of fundamental forces: finitude, decline and the general quest for meaning. Each of them draws on both external influences affecting the observable behaviour of the aged and unsubstantiated inferences about the internal processes shaping the aged self. The disjunction between these two spheres defies any notion of a contextual perspective.

Scholarly knowledge of ageing is vulnerable to implicit misconceptions rooted in a fundamental incompatibility between the language of scientific investigation and the parameters of signification among the old. One approach to fresh thinking about ageing might be to reduce these theoretical models to their basic components. A direct, simple, yet dynamic and flexible perspective on our field of interest can be based on the concepts of 'society' and 'culture', operationalized as 'control' and 'meaning'. I will argue that it is the interaction between these two coordinates of human existence that engenders the socially constituted realms of time, space and self in old age. Thus, we will examine manifestations of the metaphysical templates of time, space and self at the everyday, grass-roots level, as these are displayed in the relationships between social and personal resources (control) and goals and aspirations (meaning).

Part II

Presentations of ageing: languages of the old

5

Control: the social boundaries of age

The variety in the status of the aged in different societies is enormous. Comparative anthropological research on the aged in various cultural milieux has revealed relatively few common denominators (see, e.g., Simmons 1945; Cowgill and Holmes 1971; Myerhoff and Simic 1978; Amoss and Harell 1981a: Fry 1980; Sokolovsky 1983). Before discussing the sources of such differences, it may be useful to illustrate their range.

In hunter-gatherer societies living at the subsistence level, the conditions of daily life render the situation of the older person extremely harsh. In some tropical regions, where physical survival is ensured, social conflicts based on economic tensions are avoidable. Nevertheless, both the anthropological literature and folklore reveal the prevalence of practices such as the abandonment of the aged or their ritual killing. The aged are, in effect, sacrificed in favour of the young and fit. In some societies the old person who is no longer capable of keeping up with the group is simply left behind to perish. In others the killing of the aged is a ritual. The tribe will select individuals whose task it is to determine which of the aged are to die. These persons separate the aged from the rest of the group, provide them with a supply of foodstuffs for a number of days, and take them to an isolated location where, after a short time, they will die. In addition, there are the many reported cases of elderly persons choosing their own hour of death, such as the Eskimos retiring to the ice cap or the Japanese climbing Narayama (Sumner 1940; Simmons 1945; 1960; Fischer 1978).

In sharp contrast to these practices, in most other simple societies the acquisition of knowledge and its selective control is the key to understanding the role of the aged (Glascock and Feinman 1980). In agricultural societies and among certain nomadic herdsmen, where the knowledge and experience of the elderly are particularly valuable and the society possesses sufficient resources to continue to support them, their power is not only ensured but may even be enhanced. Indeed, in some such societies old age is a prerequisite for the position of leader, and it is the concentration of knowledge in the elders that accounts for their prestige. However, any marked deterioration in the ability to transmit personally preserved knowledge may drastically alter the social status of the aged individual to the point of excommunication (Keith 1980b).

In most contemporary urban societies, the status of the aged is equivocal. On the ideological level, society is considered responsible for the support of the aged, but socio-economic reality often stands in sharp contrast to this explicit value. Furthermore, cultural diversity makes problematic the identification of any human universe shared by all old people. The physiological-biological aspects of the ageing process are clearly insufficient to constitute such a generalization. Not only are they cross-culturally diverse in their nature and intensity – ranging from severe malnutrition to the results of advanced medical technology – but the social interpretations assigned to them vary enormously. It is therefore incumbent upon the social scientist to examine the status of the aged in different societies not from the point of view of physical health but in terms of the balance between specific socio-cultural characteristics and the general determinants of the human condition. Such efforts have varied in both general perspective and method. Perhaps the most simplistic such explanatory endeavour focuses on values, which are treated as entities with an existence of their own that can be exchanged, inculcated, internalized and adopted. Thus, some scholars (Palmore 1975) maintain that in certain societies the attitude towards the aged can be understood by reference to the cultural value of honour. Japanese society, for instance, is held to place a high value on respect for the aged, and this is treated as a fixed factor in Japanese culture overriding social or economic considerations. It is assumed that respect determines the social status of the elderly. Following this logic, if behaviour is to be explained in terms of values (Kluckhohn 1950), then there are also societies that devalue the aged. Clearly, in many cases, such a description is no more than an ethnocentric expression of our own values – an imposition on other cultures of our concepts of respect or disrespect for the aged. Even if the uniqueness of a culture is taken into account and values are traced to their origins in attitudes towards time, space and meaning, this sort of analysis lacks any reference to the social underpinnings of these values. Furthermore, even if we link reverence for the aged with the traditional society's resistance to change and disregard for the aged with progress-oriented society, the explanation remains descriptive rather than analytic. In sum, any analysis based on values is inadequate in that it does not explain the structures and processes involved in the social construction of value systems.

Another type of explanation addresses the assumed universal needs of the aged in relation to the capacity and will of a given society. Here the central problem is determining those needs. Is there any significant distinction between the needs of the aged and the needs of the rest of society? Is there an order of priority of needs? What is the relation between needs peculiar to a certain society and universal needs? In the face of these questions, anthropologists haved attempted to construct a model of basic needs appropriate for describing the situation of the aged in all societies (Cowgill and Holmes 1971). This model places at its centre the needs for nourishment, procreation and shelter, but we can imagine circumstances in which individuals may choose to forgo these. Instances of abstinence – hunger strikes, celibacy and martyrdom – undermine the absolute universality attributed to basic human needs. Furthermore, even if it is assumed that these needs are as common as they are self-evident and intelligible, there are others whose roots are clearly psychological and social, such as the needs for respect, self-respect, and social status (E. Becker 1962).

Having failed to establish a noncontroversial list of needs, it would be presumptuous to use such needs as the basis for an explanation of behaviour. Furthermore, the ascription of predetermined needs to the elderly may not only obscure the uniqueness of each person but also play into the hands of social agents interested in the orderly management of the 'problems' of the aged. It may easily become the ideological justification for viewing the old as bundles of needs requiring 'solutions'. Furthermore, this needs-oriented perspective, by establishing a static foundation for behaviour, neglects the dynamics of stimulus and response and the constantly changing nature of social action and interaction. It is little wonder that the functionalist school, based as it is on a theory of needs, is criticized for resistance to the idea of change.

Another approach to explaining ageing attempts to analyse the distribution of resources available to the aged in a given social setting by inquiring into the forms of control they exercise. It is customary, for example, to assume that in all societies knowledge and experience are highly valued resources. In our society, know-ledge is commonly acquired through learning in formal settings; life experience may even be regarded as a hindrance to such learning. Formally barred from acquiring knowledge in many institutions and informally discouraged from engaging in career-oriented courses of study, the aged are denied access to this most valuable source of social power and esteem. Special aged-oriented frame-works for learning such as universities for the Third Age (Midwinter 1984) may be intellectually, psychologically and socially beneficial, but they do not improve the status of the old in society and their integration into it. This situation stands in contrast to that of the aged in pre-literate societies; where knowledge is orally trans-mitted, the aged are equipped by the nature of their position in the social structure to control the dissemination of knowledge, thereby both preserving and even enhancing their status. Although this approach appears more reasonable than the others described above, it too fails to explain how particular social structures lend support to a particular status for the aged.

In view of this general failure, I propose that efforts to understand the variation in the status of the aged in different societies be based on an analysis of their social relationships. This analysis distin-guishes two ideal types of social structure: 'simple society' and 'complex society' (see Kuper 1988). The measures of simplicity and complexity do not represent any attribution of a particular menta-lity (primitive or modern, irrational or rational), hierarchically juxtaposed, but constitute an abstract structural continuum along which concrete examples of social milieux can be located. In the following I will attempt to demonstrate how such a perspective can be of assistance in understanding the situation of the aged in different societies without recourse either to ascribed needs or to value systems.

The first structural dimension to be mapped is the relative strength and cohesiveness of social relationships. This measure distinguishes social settings in terms of whether relationships are simple or multifaceted and the extent to which they interlock. In a simple society relationships are multifaceted. Interpersonal commitments are underwritten by the co-existence and interdependence of kinship bonds that are simultaneously economic ties, religious associations, political obligations, and community interests. As a result, the basic social unit is one in which consumption cannot be divorced from production and economic responsibility is linked to ritual and the maintenance of the moral order. Thus, the defence of the social unit is contingent upon the fulfilment of familial duties, and deviant behaviour is controlled by lifelong and comprehensive knowledge of both accuser and accused. The domains of family, politics, law, religion, and the economy are inseparable. Hence, individuals rarely break ties in any one realm, since this would have repercussions on all others. In contrast, in a complex society most social relationships are single-stranded. Subsistence is primarily dependent upon links to financial and employment frameworks (but cf. Douglas and Isherwood 1978), and, although personal ties may develop around this relationship, when the relationship ceases to exist these subsidiary ties generally dissolve.

Social relations in simple societies have considerable strength not because people in such societies have stronger feelings but because the social structure creates stronger ties of obligation and loyalty. The members of a social unit lack alternatives, and social boundaries often correspond with territorial ones, thus preventing free passage from one social unit to another. In contemporary Western society, in contrast, numerous alternatives are open to the individual. Having lost one's job, for example, one can usually find another and satisfy the same economic needs without significant repercussions for family and community ties.

The second structural dimension of old people's lives to be mapped is the social division of labour. In most simple societies, the basic determinants of the organization of social life are gender and age. These characteristics are dependent not on the desires of individuals or on their ability and talents but on biological factors. To a certain extent, age is more amenable to manipulation than gender (though some studies indicate that it too may be subject to social negotiation (Erikson 1950; Garfinkel 1967a: 116–85). As society becomes more complex, the division of labour is increasingly determined by special skills, and the social and economic rewards for the development of these skills in turn foster further specialization. In simple societies, although some individuals may master special technical and ceremonial knowledge, a special career is not the dominant aspect of most life courses. In contrast, in complex societies, apart from certain periods – of which early youth and old age constitute the most promiment examples – the division of labour is based on expertise.

The third structural dimension by which complex and simple societies are distinguished is the range of social groups with which individuals are linked. This dimension is in effect a function of the two dimensions discussed above. In complex societies there is a wide variety of groups to which individuals may belong, the extent of involvement in them ranging from full integration and identification to partial and temporary commitment. Shifting involvements are also an important characteristic of the structure of complex societies. A person may change occupation, family set-up, or political allegiance. The relative independence this implies is not necessarily freedom, for it is often accompanied by anonymity, alienation and fragmentation of identity. The implication of such a social structure for the aged may be the gradual weakening and possible abrupt disruption and disappearance of their connections with others, eroding their identity and increasing their dependency on the institutionalized social environment. Thus, in old age, when one may in fact require more support than ever, family and friends may be replaced by bureaucratic agencies offering formal, one-sided relationships. In simple societies, in contrast, the social structure grounds the aged in mutual loyalties and obligations to a community. Differences in the status of old people in different simple societies are attributable not to cultural values attached to ageing but to the particular condition.

The organization of social life combines elements that are thought of as flexible and potentially subject to transformation, and elements considered predetermined or 'natural', such as gender and race. Age, entailing both transformation and continuity, contains a host of paradoxes and conflicts. These incongruities will serve as the focus for the following examination of the relationship between ageing and social structure (see Steward 1976; Baxter and Almagor 1978; Keith 1980b; Kertzer and Keith 1984; Bernardi 1985).

Age is generally perceived as something external, 'out there', by which our experiences are shaped, but this perception is self-contradictory. On the one hand, age is seen as predetermined – it is spoken of in terms of milestones, events such as birthdays that are clearly marked on the calendar. On the other hand, age is construed as a constant process of change divided into discrete units of reference by arbitrary social structuring. In other words, age is conceived of in both absolute and relative terms. In determining that an individual is of a certain age, we relate to this age as if it were an absolute, involving fixed expectations, roles and identities. Age-related norms have a major influence on the formation of our attitudes towards ourselves and others, to the extent that by reference to age alone we can conjure up a mental picture of a social person. Reference to a given age, however, is also made up of meaning specific to the culture and the society and in terms of a life expectancy which varies greatly from one population to another. The relativity of age is further emphasized in social settings where time reckoning is based not on numerical ordering but on the assignment of a point in time to one event in relation to another. In these instances, concepts such as 'before' and 'after' may replace a fixed locus within a pre-ordained sequence. Furthermore, since behaviour, appearance, mental and physical capacity, and social standing all serve as insignia of age, different societies may attribute age-images differently.

The concept of age, then, has internal contradictory dimensions. The first is its being one of the most commonly accepted criteria for social evaluation and location. Using lower and upper age limits, we identify what is 'permitted' or 'forbidden'. Between the two limits is a range of age-related behaviour that can be viewed as one level of an age-based system of social stratification. The age of marriage, for example, is formally determined only at the lower limit. This legal limit reflects the lack of correspondence between sexual and social maturity. Where eligibility for marriage is established by puberty, such a limit may seem odd. The age of marriage also has an upper limit, effected not by law but by symbolic-cultural references. Thus, for example, a wide age difference between spouses when one of them is of an advanced age is invariably the subject of curiosity and gossip.

Age boundaries are enforced by means of both formal laws and social sanctions. For example, compulsory education requires children to participate in the state-controlled age-grade system known as schooling. The same may be said of almost every aspect of our lives, since all legal systems set up upper and lower age limits within which responsibilities, eligibilities, and even viabilities (such as that of the foetus in the case of abortion) are established and legitimated. Social relationships, therefore, are also shaped and regulated by these rules, which establish age-related arenas for action and interaction. The obvious example is retirement, which in many instances is mandatory. Even if the law upholds the right of an individual to choose the time of termination of working life, trade-union agreements, pension schemes, and, most important, social pressures compel most people to retire at a predetermined age. In settings whose structure resembles that of simple societies, such as family businesses, self-employment, or guild-like associations, these pressures may be modified and retirement age rendered more flexible. With regard to professional life, then, while retirement constitutes the upper age limit, entry into the labour market is also established by law. In addition to age boundaries formalized within the legal system, there are unwritten rules that prove far more difficult to analyse. It is considered incongruous, for example, for a young person (either in terms of chronological age or in terms of appearance) to hold a top executive position; we do not expect the young to possess the abilities deemed appropriate to a 'proper' executive. In this case, age serves as the principal yardstick by which such abilities are measured.

The powerful stereotypical force of age-related attributes may be found in those cases where the age barrier is trespassed. Such is the case of elderly students, for example. Despite the fact that universities do not set an upper age limit to the admission of students, they are perceived as institutions populated principally by and for young people. The presence of an older student at university is often regarded as puzzling, an attitude deriving from the perception that the university is part of one's social and professional career. A person is deemed to enter university, not only to acquire knowledge for its own sake, but also to embark on a career. Why a person would want to attend an educational institution without the concomitant professional advantages is unclear and hence, the presence of an older person, whose working life is over, appears contradictory, if not subversive of the image of the university as an arena for the advancement of the young. Furthermore, the campus 'youth' culture may be seen as unfitting and unbecoming for the 'needs', 'mentality' and, indeed, very presence of an old person. The emergence of universities for the Third Age as age-homogenous settings provide further evidence of the unease attendant on the presence of older students at regular universities.

In contrast to the belief that biological factors such as sex and age are gradually losing their significance in our society, there is practically no social role which does not entail some kind of age boundary. If society is a series of steps, age is one of the primary factors affecting the shift from one step to another. This is very clear in simple societies, where social relations and social structure are organized to a large extent according to membership in age-grades (M. Wilson 1951), but is no less important in complex ones. We have already touched upon what is perhaps the most extreme example of the phenomenon – the education system. Although there are exceptional cases, generally speaking progress in school is determined by chronological age, and the structure of the school itself is based on a fixed and predetermined age order. In terms of differential talent and learning ability, however, there would appear to be no justification for simply placing children of the same age in the same class. Indeed, in some social settings, either by force of circumstance, as in the case of remote, sparsely inhabited areas, or as an expression of an ideology of literacy, as in the Jewish *yeshiva*, this pattern is broken and challenged.

The ascribed correlation between ability and membership in an age-group loses its force between the ages of twenty and fifty and re-emerges at the end of life, when age stereotypes once again play an essential role in the stratification process. Army officers and policemen, for example, are expected to retire earlier than clerks, the assumption being that the characteristics and abilities required for their particular occupations are subject to gradual erosion as they approach their mid-fifties. Athletes are perhaps the most extreme case, since their physical abilities reach a competitive peak relatively early. Scientists too, particularly in the exact sciences, are generally deemed to have exhausted their productivity prior to midlife. On the other hand, for some professionals, such as lawyers, clergymen, politicians, and academics, retirement is relatively late. In these instances life experience is conceived of as a resource, the value of which increases in the direct proportion to age and which may only be undermined by the onset of 'senility'.

The second dimension of the concept of age is its significance for everyday relationships, situations, and discourses. Age stereotypes, the most obvious of which is appearance, are all-pervasive. Clothing, countenance, posture, hair colour and style, and a host of other visible features all convey an age-related image with social connotations and implications for attitudes and behaviour. Thus, while at a particular age a person is permitted to be frivolous, at another this same conduct is severely sanctioned; wisdom, equanimity and level-headedness are the privilege of yet another age-group. Those who do not comply with these preconceptions may find themselves subject to unremitting social criticism.

How does age contribute to the construction of social relationships? First of all, as we have seen, the importance of age as a unit of information in social communication varies in different periods of the life course. During youth and old age it is extremely salient, while in other periods it is somewhat less so (though it may arise in particular situations, especially those in which knowledge of the other person is limited). Second, the importance of age varies with the type of relationship. In some contexts, such as formal bureaucratic relations, it is in the foreground. In others, such as intimate relations, it is of secondary importance. Third, when people refer to age it is not always clear whether they mean chronological, emotional, functional, or social age. A person is considered old by virtue of chronological age, and this dimension continues to dominate age definition until the end of life. Although chronological age constantly changes, it is socially defined as static. The fine internal differentiations between various stages of ageing such as the 'young old' and the 'old old' may occupy the minds of experts but have no bearing on the immutable umbrella concept of 'old age'. As the link between social age and chronological age gradually dissolves, this single negative identity denies the possibility that old people may undergo change. Age becomes an embedded feature of every relationship and situation in which elderly people find themselves – an indelible property which cannot be eliminated, ignored or disguised.

Age is thus both an overt form of social control and a tacit device of manipulation and regulation pervading all areas of life. The state of being old can be understood in terms of the workings of such social mechanisms, and, as we have seen, it is characterized by decreasing resources. Yet control alone cannot account for the uniqueness of ageing. It is transformations in meaning that, together with structural changes, constitute the experienced reality of later life.

6

Meaning: the cultural boundaries of life

Every society has its own particular images of human life. In some mythologies the life of a human being is described in terms of the image of a snake biting its own tail or a dragon swallowing itself (see Eliade 1967). In a classic riddle put to Oedipus, man is described as a creature that crawls on all fours and then walks on two legs and finally on three. These different images manifest both a process, the life course, and a cycle – eternal return, ashes to ashes, dust to dust, the circadian rhythms of body time, the reiteration of festivals and daily routines. The constant interplay between the meaning we attach to the progressive flow of time and the omnipresence of cyclical time constitute two dimensions of human life which may be termed 'course' and 'cycle' respectively.

There are two principal ways of understanding the human life course or cycle: by examining it as a structure made up of different stages and by focusing on one point in time from which situations and contexts can be identified and interpreted. The first of these perspectives may be compared to a map of the life journey. It determines in advance not only the course of a life but also its critical choices. This approach is somewhat simplistic in its attribution of a universal character to life stages, ignoring motivation, personal world view, and specific circumstances. Furthermore, while most such orientations take into account childhood and youth, they overlook ageing. Thus the prevailing approaches in psychology argue for a correlation between biological development and psychological change, with an emphasis on psychosexual transitions. The most widely discussed example is the Freudian psychoanalytic perspective, which has given rise to a variety of attempts to examine the psychodynamics of human development over time. Some scholars have argued that age sixty-five marks the onset of a biological and psychological regression which leads to social withdrawal. This withdrawal may manifest itself as either a sense of lack of fulfilment and failure or a sense of self-realization. The concept of a psychological trajectory of crises is most fully realized in the work of Erikson (1950), for whom the eighth and final stage of the life cycle, influenced by illness and other malfunctions, involves the recognition of the end of life and approaching death. In this stage, the person may either experience an integration of the 'self' or, alternatively, sink into despair.

Another theory of the life course or cycle draws on the relationship between internal development and control over reality. It traces the changes experienced in the course of a life in terms of mastery of resources and maintains that there is a curvelike pattern of gradual change in such mastery from high dependency at infancy through an increase in control in youth and adulthood to the final decline that comes with ageing. This gradual loss of control is expressed in regressive fantasies, retreat and the absence of instrumentalism. According to this approach, the influence of the external environment on the life course is minimal; what is significant and causative is psychological development.

Other theoretical approaches address the influence on the life course of factors originating in society and culture. Functionalism, discussed earlier in connection with disengagement theory, assumes the existence of a socially sketched map for the individual life. Roles and the social relationships emerging from them are seen as expressions of the requirements of the society within which the individual lives. The culture-and-personality approach argues that personality is moulded by culture.

The critical problem with all these perspectives is the interpretation of the shift from one life stage to another. In simple societies such transitions are accomplished by means of symbolic practices called 'rites of passage' (Van Gennep 1969 [1908]; Turner 1969) through which persons exchange one social identity for another. Rites of passage are composed of three stages: separation of individuals from their environment, transformation of their identity, and reintegration into society with a newly acquired status. The middle stage may continue for days or even longer, during which time the initiates perform a series of tasks and are exposed in an intensive and concentrated way to the key symbols and central myths of their culture, often through acts of overt sacrilege. On the completion of this stage they are returned to their society bearing the insignia of a new status and functioning within the frame of their novel identities.

Rites of passage are rare in our own fragmented societies (i.e., characterized by multifaceted, interlocking relationships) though they are to be found in situations that are structurally similar to simple societies, such as in total institutions (hospitals, prisons or military camps). Retirement from work might be conceived as such a rite of passage inasmuch as it may involve the ceremonial and often humiliating separation from a previous identity, but it confers no alternative identity, no social future.

The second approach to understanding the life course or cycle is in terms of subjective reminiscing rather than structural factors. This is regarded as a mechanism for the construction of the 'self'. This process involves the adoption of principles of selection by which apparently cherished memories are shaped by filtering, processing, and feedback. People write or relate their life histories to present particular images that they are interested in sharing, promoting, and preserving. The same is true of the day-to-day recollections of old people as they apply techniques of modification and adjustment to enhance their chances of survival. The dearth of resources at their disposal compels them to use to the utmost all the means they can muster. Carefully constructed self-presentation to serve immediate ends is one such strategy (see Johnson 1976; Myerhoff 1978a; 1982; Myerhoff and Tufte 1975; Bertaux 1981; Rosemayr 1981; Langness and Frank 1987; Hareven and Adams 1982; Frank and Vanderburgh 1986). In this approach the life cycle is not fixed but changes from situation to situation in accordance with differing interpretations of the needs of the individual and the social partners to whom the presentation is addressed.

This orientation is based on the increasingly prevalent assumption in the psychology, anthropology and sociology of ageing that the individual endeavours to establish a sense of life-long continuity, a personal life course the components of which are controlled and connected by an experiential, emotional thread. Thus the haphazard, inconsistent, multidimensional events of a life are framed and organized to project a consistent, self-justifying story that makes sense and conveys meaning. Such depictions may be employed in the reconstruction of ethnic identities, the search for roots, and the affirmation of social and political allegiances. The reinforcement of ethnic symbolism in old age can be construed either as a cultural recourse to a source of identity in a state of social invisibility or as an attempt to re-establish lost networks and regain social support founded on common identification with an ageless set of shared values. Thus, returning to formative experiences or to a prior time of meaningful social involvement, such as boarding school, college, or army days, may serve the construction of a coherent identity, often alongside other identities. Sometimes, as in the case of old boys' networks, such attachments are fuelled by common vested interests and sustained by ongoing commitments. The 'cohort effect' – the indelible impact of a shared historical experience (such as the American economic depression of the 1920s, the Holocaust, or World War I) – is another example of the penetration of the present by the past (see Elder 1974; Hareven 1978). Some research (Gubrium and Lynott 1983; Hazan 1983), however, has demonstrated that a substantial portion of the behaviour of older people is not necessarily guided by any notion of continuity. On the contrary, the primary operating principle in old people's temporal orientation may be the desire to break from the past.

All these approaches rest on the relativist assumption that everything connected to age and the life cycle is subject to individual, social, and cultural variation. One phenomenon regarded as absolute, however, is death. Generally speaking, death is seen as the conclusion of the life course, the cessation of biological, social and mental life. Any notion of death which does not correspond to the corporeal end of the life course is viewed as disturbing, since it signals a situation in which the various dimensions of the life course no longer inform one another. In a society in which chronology is basic to the structuring of experience and knowledge, the fragmentation of the life course may prove disruptive not only for the individual but for social life itself. Barriers against death are constantly erected and defended in the form of taboos such as avoidance of contamination by the corpse, territorial segregation of cemeteries, and avoidance of the dying or, alternatively, preoccupation with death. Indeed, ageing itself may be viewed as such a barrier in that it is commonly thought of as the final stage prior to inevitable death. In simple societies, accusation of witchcraft generally implies an association with death because witchcraft is seen to contain elements of chaos – the breakdown of barriers to death. In complex societies, where explicit accusation of witchcraft is absent, old age may well serve the same purpose. This is manifest in the fact, for instance, that the aged are exiled to institutions.

The separation of the aged from society, the identification of ageing with ugliness, evil, and horror, and the reluctance to engage in physical contact with the aged all indicate that ageing is perceived as a dangerous area located, as it were, between life and death. These phenomena are also prevalent amongst the aged themselves, often even more apparent because of their own proximity to death. On the whole, the non-aged do not distinguish between the 'old old' and the 'young old' as gerontologists recommend, but such fine distinctions are made by the aged themselves, many of whom are very particular about grading themselves above others whose appearance, functioning and health appear to fall short of their own. Indeed, research shows (Hochschild 1973) that the aged always identify others as older and therefore closer to death than they. The same principle holds true for the non-aged, who see the aged as separating them from the disturbing yet unavoidable taboo-riddled phenomenon of death.

In other societies there is no such imperative nexus between death and the aged. In medieval Europe, where the infant mortality rate was high, death was associated more with children than the aged. The giving of names to children, for instance, was delayed until an age when they were presumed to have attained viability; only then were they viewed as human beings (Ariès 1965). Because of disease, war, and malnutrition, it was the non-aged population that constituted the bulk of mortality, and the possibility of death accompanied the individual throughout the life course. Finally, the small portion of the aged in the overall population contributed to a dissociation between old age and death (Ariès 1983). What is at issue, therefore, is the specific cultural meaning attached to the connection between physical death and chronological time. In order to understand this we must distinguish between death as the end point of biological existence and death as the termination of social life. There is no necessary synchronization between these two different types of death, and the relation between them may take various forms (Palgi and Abramovitz 1984). In complex societies, social death precedes biological death. A person begins to lose social roles and cultural identity prior to the termination of biological existence. The interval between social death and physical death may span a period of many years, and it is one of the fundamental elements of our culture in relation to the aged.

Cultural attitudes towards biological and social death are manifest in three areas: preparation for death, the possibility of life after death, and links between the living and the dead. Among the Alaskan Eskimos it was customary for a man to fix the day of his own death. He would tell his life story to his family, pray, instruct fellow tribesmen on matters considered important, and then leave the tribe to meet his death in the barren wastes of the ice cap (Graburn 1969; Freuchen 1961). Among the peoples of northern Siberia, a man determined the date of his death, which was then ceremonially administered by his first-born son (de Beauvoir 1975: chapter 2). Among the Dinka of the Upper Nile, priests were buried alive on their own initiative and with the participation of the population, who believed that only through such burial would the soul of the deceased reach the world of the ancestors (Simmons 1960).

In certain societies it was customary to bury living creatures – such as animals and even humans of the deceased's household – together with the dead. The cultural assumption underlying such customs was that the biological cessation of life was temporary and life in its physical fullness was bound to resume. A similar correspondence between social and somatic life prevails when social demise and biological decay co-occur in a culturally constructed process of decline. Among the Merina people of Madagascar, a temporary burial takes place several months before the final one (Bloch 1971), and between the two burials the deceased is considered still part of the community: his wife is not allowed to remarry, his children are obliged to display respect for him, and his property is viewed as still belonging to him. Hence, the deceased continues to be socially alive, despite the fact that his physical presence is no more. This delayed final interment permits a gradual transition from life to death for the deceased and for those left behind. An entirely different approach to the question of life after death is manifested in the destruction of all relics and memories of the dead, which gives expression to their absolute exile from the world of the living (Hertz 1960 (1928)). In other circumstances, often in the same societies, the mark of the deceased is preserved both socially and materially. Burial, for instance, may take place in or near the homestead, and the body may be preserved for embalmment. The remains of the deceased, believed to represent and embody the spirit and to be a sign of continuing significant as a social being, serve as a focus for worship. A shrine built around them may become the centre of religious activity whereby the living propitiate the spirits of their ancestors (Bloch and Parry 1982).

This ambivalence towards the dead, expressed, on the one hand, in their determined obliteration and, on the other, in the zealous preservation of their memory, is prevalent in many cultures, including our own. It reflects the chaos perceived to follow death and the undermining of the capacity to organize reality anew. Mourning rituals are a cultural recipe for coping with the cognitive and emotional perplexity caused by death. Ambiguous situations, of which death is a prime example, evoke cultural responses which draw their main elements from the domain of the sacred and profane (Douglas 1966). The death ceremonies of the Nyakyusa in Tanzania, for example, are pervaded by symbols of dirt and madness and behaviour which under ordinary circumstances would be strictly avoided. During the ceremonies people smear themselves with human waste, masturbate in public, and generally behave as if they had taken leave of their senses (M. Wilson 1951). This association between cultural disarray and death is most salient in the liminal stage of rites of passage.

A striking instance of continuing links with the world of the dead is ancestor worship. In many societies, the worlds of the dead and the living are perceived as parallel to and informing one another. The living communicate with the dead through prayer and sacrifice which they hope will bring them good fortune. Pertinent to our discussion is the fact that it is the aged who are often thought to be closest to the world of the dead and, by virtue of this proximity, to possess supernatural powers.

Family genealogies are traced in all societies, including our own, as a means of creating a thread of descent linking us with our forefathers. In the United States, for example, there are services which trace family histories and engage in searches for lost kin. These investigations usually serve no instrumental purpose but are used in the construction of personal identity. In a society in which cultural heritage is often either unknown or tenuous, weaving oneself into the fabric of social space and time takes on special importance. The mystical properties of such links and lineages evoke the sense that one's ancestors originated in mythical times. Similarly, the identification of a culture's mythical figures with its elders may be seen to bestow upon the latter the attributes of the former. The case of the establishment of new nations, whose founding fathers are their current political leaders, attests to this phenomenon; the creation of religious cults revolving around such figures is commonplace. Israeli culture, with its living pantheon of founding fathers alongside a growing population of aged leaders, is an interesting example (Hazan 1987a).

Disruption of the proper but fragile boundary between the living and the dead is commonly regarded as dangerous. Ghosts, for instance, may be deemed to be the product of faulty and improper burial ceremonies which compel the restless spirits of the dead to return to the world of the living in the form of evil beings. This same ambiguity may be seen to underlie the phenomenon of spirit possession, for example, the Jewish dybbuk and the Caribbean zombie. Most cultures have strategies such as exorcism for limiting the influence of such beings.

In some societies, a third category intervenes between the categories of the living and the dead. This category, which may be termed the 'living dead' (Keith 1980a), is represented by aged persons who are mentally inept. One response to such persons is witchcraft accusations against them; others are separation from the community, expulsion from the tribe, or simply abandonment. Even if the old are allowed to remain within their community, as in our society, their status as human beings remains ambiguous. Avoidance, separation and charitable and patronizing protectiveness are all manifestations of this ambiguity.

The numerous and varied endeavours to perpetuate existence beyond biological life testify to the fact that the boundary between the living and the dead is perceived as permeable. Symbolic immortalization – including the preservation of personal photographs and family heirlooms, the writing of books, the planting of trees, the erection of gravestones and construction of monuments, and procreation itself – constitutes an attempt to perpetuate life beyond death (Lifton 1977; E. Becker 1973).

Another kind of effort to cross the thin line separating the living from the dead and simulate the after-life is entering a state in which chronological time loses its grip over daily existence. It is commonly assumed that, by virtue of its proximity, the fear of death increases with age. There is, however, evidence that elderly people are no more afraid of death than people in other age-groups and that it is in middle age, when awareness of one's mortality surfaces, that fear of death is strongest (Kalish 1976). This finding may be explained in at least two ways. It could be argued that what is actually being studied is not fear of death at all but its rationalization. Since death is so close, the aged person develops a particular mechanism of self-defence by way of denial – expressed, for example, in concentration on the present concerns of day-to-day life and on separation from the past and indifference to the future. A second explanation is that in fact the elderly person enters a different time universe in which the thought of impending death loses its significance. In a revealing example, one of the members of a day centre for Jewish elderly people in California (Myerhoff 1978b), was determined to celebrate his ninety-fifth birthday. He was well aware that his death was imminent, and, although his doctors maintained that his hours were numbered he insisted on going ahead with the celebration, which he attended connected to an oxygen tank. During the party, he announced that he was donating a sum of money so that the other members of the day centre could continue celebrating his birthday until he reached the age of one hundred. He did not mention his impending death. When he had finished his speech he was taken to a side room, where he died. This event had an enormous impact on everyone present. Clearly the man wished to think in terms of time after his biological death, and he succeeded in fulfilling his desire in the most practical sense by guaranteeing the continued celebration of his birthday long after his physical departure.

In effect, this phenomenon reverses the relations between social and biological death. Whereas our society establishes social death as the precursor of physiological demise, the elderly, by attempting to perpetuate their cultural existence, exchange the two. In this situation, social structure no longer informs the experience of ageing, and defiance of social consensus produces a sense of liberation. The new meanings infused into the vacuum between social and somatic deaths may be culturally innovative and individually rewarding. To understand the conditions under which such reconstruction of life may occur, the unique nature of the temporal universe of the aged, engendered by particular permutations of the balance between control and meaning, must be explored.

7

Another universe: time, space, and self

The social patterning of time, which originates in the inability to conceptualize a continuous flow of change, may take various forms. Cultural codes breaking up time into symbolically recognizable units serve to make sense of experience. When these codes lose their social validity or cease to reflect experience, temporal construction collapses. Ageing is commonly measured in terms of chronological indices, as a continuum of events over a period of time. In fact, however, the concept of linear progression which underlies the world of the non-aged is irrelevant and inapplicable to the reality of old age and is therefore replaced by the aged themselves with more suitable temporal orientations. The central problem confronted by elderly persons is not role relinquishment, functioning, social others, or the stereotypes and social images in which they find themselves entrapped, but disordered time.

The time universe of the aged is shot through with paradox. We have seen that ageing is commonly perceived as a static condition with the aged as its unchanging inhabitants. This perception expresses itself in the various solutions proposed for the socially ascribed problems of the aged; though the needs of the aged are provided for, there is no mechanism allowing for their development. Among the non-aged, moving from one stage of life to another, the opportunity for socially approved transformations is a culturally cherished privilege. The old, however, are not supposed to change as others do and, accordingly, are denied such opportunity. This structural immobility stands in absolute contradiction to their personal experience and sensibility, for they are in fact under-

74

going rapid and important changes in roles, identities, abilities and bodily functions that influences their self-perception and their capacity to handle everyday affairs.

This disorder in the time universe of the aged is a consequence of the discrepancy between desires (material or ideal) and the meaning people attribute to their existence, on the one hand, and the capacity to bring these under control, on the other.[1] The tension between means and ends, control and meaning, engenders a dynamic that shapes the framework of values called 'progress'. We move from one stage of controllable meaning to an ensuing stage of meaning for which some measure of mastery is deemed possible. In the course of this constant quest for attainable meaning, a complex system of checks and balances emerges. This system is legitimated by social institutions and cultural conventions which discourage deviance and the disorderly progression associated with unrealistic visions or delusions. Those who, for whatever reason, fail to comply with this controlled equation between means and ends are labelled misfits – delinquent, mentally disturbed or culturally inept. Methods of correction, rehabilitation, education and readaptation are designed to restore order and synchronization.[2]

In simple societies such tensions are virtually non-existent, since there is almost no gap between reality and what is needed to improve it (J. Henry 1963: Introduction). On the whole, people consume what they produce and produce only what they need to consume. For a multitude of reasons, the dynamic which drives progress in our own society does not exist: simple technology does not allow for storage and transportation of food products, control over nature is limited, there is no market economy, and specialization is absent from the division of labour. Hence, anthropologists have characterized 'traditional' society as resistant to change. Clearly, from the point of view of daily life, this designation is meaningless. There are constant changes, among them war, epidemics and famine, often with a dramatic impact on the life of the community. Such changes do not, however, engender social progress. These societies are therefore considered devoid of historical perspective or, in Lévi-Strauss's (1967) terms, 'cold' as opposed to 'hot'. The particular situation of the aged person in such a society is no different to that of others; it is determined, as it were, by the relatively static character of the society as a whole. Anthropological research has illuminated the time universe of 'cold' and 'hot' societies (Hallowell 1937; Hall 1984; Maxwell 1972; Leach 1971; Zerubavel 1985), but only a few attempts have been made to explain the nexus between social structure and the cultural codes in which temporal perspectives originate (see, e.g., Doob 1971; Evans-Pritchard 1939; Roth 1962; Roy 1959; Zerubavel 1982). I propose that temporal perspectives may be explained with reference to the balance struck between meaning and control. Furthermore, I will venture to analyse this time universe *vis-à-vis* its locus of emergence, namely the self of the aged person. This analysis rests on the premise that the self is always both a temporally-bound and a time-binding process; self-consciousness provides the mechanism by which time may be experienced, constructed or even arrested, since awareness of time fundamentally involves self-awareness – that is, recognition of one's place within the present moment *vis-à-vis* one's place in other possible moments, past or future (Wells and Stryker 1988: 222).

In our society, the connection between the aged's universe of meaning and their ability to control it is disrupted. The social agencies designed to help them bridge the gap between the two existential dimensions no longer operate. On the one hand, the aged are seen as being at a social standstill; on the other, the changes occurring in their lives are extraordinarily rapid and extreme. There is nothing to moderate, balance, or mediate between the two, and, consequently, tension mounts.

Children are expected to follow a coordinated path of biological, emotional, intellectual, and social development. Institutionalized mechanisms of social control, such as the family and the school system, are designed to ensure that this co-ordination is maintained. Sanctions are applied against children who attempt to break away from these regulated tracks, and where punishment is ineffective they may be transferred to settings designed to accommodate exceptionally slow or rapid mental development. These frameworks restore the workings of the social clock to 'normality' – synchronized socialization. In the case of the aged, such support mechanisms are entirely lacking.

Disengagement theory argues that one way to redress the balance between expectations and ability is disengagement from the social environment. Notwithstanding the harsh criticism levelled against this theory, it should be noted to its credit that it does recognize the gulf between resources and desires. Similarly, other theoretical approaches explicitly or implicitly employ the notion of the relationship between means and ends as a key to the understanding of ageing (see Teski 1979b; Thomae 1970). However, the repercussions of the discrepancies inherent in the temporal universe of the aged have not been considered. It could be argued that since the source of the temporal disorder is socio-structural, it is not amenable to correction at the personal level. However, from the point of view of the aged person, it may lead to behavioural chaos, inability to comprehend reality, moral crisis, a crisis of trust and deep depression, and the need to take action is therefore pressing. The various possible responses may logically and empirically be divided into four types.

The first of these responses is abandonment of any attempt at control. Psychologists term this strategy 'retreat' or 'withdrawal'. Elderly people, finding themselves incapable of maintaining a link between their dwindling resources and ability, on the one hand, and the universe of meaning, on the other, simply abandon their resources and, through self-induced thoughts and feelings, invest all their remaining strength in a world of meaning still within their control. Choosing disengagement from social life, they may conjure up an imaginary world of dreams and fantasies. In this case, disengagement is a prerequisite for the mastery of meaning because it forestalls unwelcome intrusions. Persons in this situation may sink into self-imposed isolation and consequently be placed in institutions for the 'mentally frail' elderly, where they can pursue their withdrawal to the point of almost total abandonment of control. Not only is it now legitimated by the social label applied to them, but they are encouraged and rewarded for being docile and apparently co-operative.

A second way of coping with the discrepancy between meaning and control is the exact opposite of the one just described: abandonment of any attempt to maintain and acquire meaning in favour of control. Values, identities, beliefs and moral codes are suppressed or ignored, and immediate gratification of daily wants becomes a central principle. The frame of mind associated with this pattern of adjustment involves fatalism, cynicism and irony. On occasion all of these are expressed in a violation of social norms identified as pathological. The cantankerous old person acts in blatant defiance of social conceptions concerning the elderly. Our inability to control these elderly people makes us view them as irrational, and we tend to explain them away as suffering illnesses associated with old age.

A third technique for dealing with the discrepancy between meaning and control is the abandonment of both. This is effectively the loss of the desire to live, and it may find expression in a variety of ways. The elderly may stop eating and, if not discovered in time, die of disease and malnutrition. In other cases, they may suddenly die following retirement or entry into an institutional setting.

A final pattern of coping is the attempt to strike a new balance between control and meaning either by adjusting meaning to the available field of control or by renewal of meaning. The elderly may concentrate on things which they are still able and permitted to master – daily routines, hobbies, volunteer work and personal and domestic chores, all activities which are of no consequence to the social environment and do not challenge their disengagement. Thus they maintain control of units of meaning which have hitherto occupied only a marginal place in their lives. Scant attention has been paid in the socio-anthropological literature to the performance of behaviour which appears to serve no purpose, but observations of the old and other socially suspended persons reveal that such repetitive behavioural routines are followed fanatically. Again, these addictive behaviours are conveniently interpreted as forms of compulsive-obsessive mental aberration to be treated accordingly, but they may be more realistically seen as an attempt to limit the existential world to activities over which control is possible. In research conducted in England, some old people justified their refusal to enter old-age homes on the grounds that they would no longer be able to prepare a cup of tea for themselves (Hazan 1987b). Clearly they were not referring to the drinking of the tea, which they would certainly be able to do in the institution; rather, they were implying that in entering the institution they would be losing control of this last solitary area of cultural sanctuary. This suggests that custom and habit serve to connect an individual to past and future. Through constant repetition the elderly person re-enacts the past, thus maintaining and reinforcing an identity and at the same time denying access to change or decline. The repetitive perform-ance of activities creates a sense of security based on changeless reality. The simple act of drinking tea serves to halt the march of time by implying that what was, is and will remain the same.

Rather than preserving attachments to previous forms, the aged may seek new meaning which, in conjunction with the ability to control it, gives them a new reason for living. I have already discussed the most obvious manifestations of this response, such as the retirement communities, with their own novel cultural systems of symbols and decision making. Individual solutions in the same vein include adopting a new activity which represents an entirely fresh start. In these instances, old people may exploit their relative freedom from occupational and familial commitments in order to embark on new ventures involving new sources of meaning.

In all these modes of adjustment we are witness to a shift from a concept of time as flowing in one linear direction – the dominant temporal dimension in the lives of the non-aged – to a cyclical notion of time. Time may be entirely a matter of subjective evalu-ation. Cherished memories may become a pivotal time-structuring device, and momentary gestures of affect and sympathy may fill the old person's life with infinite joy. Conversely, tedious routines are liable to be forgotten or dismissed as of no consequence. The unlimited flexibility of the cognitive-emotional construction of time suggests that the experience of time must be analytically separated from the reckoning system whereby it is measured. This is par-ticularly important with reference to old age, when markers and signifiers are divorced from signified and significance (Barthes 1977; Sperber 1975). Mythlike, self-sustained temporal units may be the focus of meaning without being reflected in observable reality, and the expressions of time which make up the aged's language of communication with others may be of no importance to their inner selves and reveal nothing about them.

This suggested split in the temporal universe of the aged draws on the distinction proposed by Ricoeur between the two dimen-sions of human time – the personal and the public, the personally mortal and the socially communicable (Klemm 1983). This distinction generates two types of cultural narrative. One addresses the invisible audience of significant others whose presence is conditional upon neither current time nor defined territory. It is not dialogical but reflective, a self-told story relevant and meaningful to the narrator. In some respects, this form of self-communication has the properties of myth as described by Mason (1980: 16) in that it

has a structure, an architecture, a plot consisting of critical dimensions and plausible changing perspective. It also has a way of growing within and being completed by oneself, yet it is guided by others previously involved in it from remote times and places who know it as their own. It brings us across such artificial distances as time and space to these others, it translates us from ourselves to them. To some it seems dreamlike and fantastic, though its structure remains orderly through its subtle transformations. Time accelerates and slows, condenses and elongates, just as space envelops and shrinks.

In contrast, narrative communication with non-significant others is regulated by symbolic representations which juxtapose distant worlds of meaning (Leach 1976; Holy and Stuchlik 1983) and is formulated in terms of socially acceptable temporal frameworks. This form of narrative serves as the basis of dialogue and public rhetoric (Fisher 1987). It enables people to live their everyday lives and is not necessarily fused with the reflective narrative of personal myth.

The manipulation of time just described is by no means drug-induced. Rather, it is a rational response to an inescapable socio-cultural condition, and as such it might be expected to extend beyond the personal psychological enterprise to the domain of social support and reinforcement among the aged themselves. Indeed, research indicates that in non-coercive age-homogeneous settings for the old, a social system which reflects and fosters temporal manipulations such as a split between inner and external time or the creation of a present-bound reality may very well emerge (Myerhoff 1978a; Hazan 1980a).

Trapped between life and death, personal experience and social time, old people occupy a unique cultural-symbolic space (see Rowles and Ohta 1981; Gubrium 1972). The demarcation line between the aged and society, the phenomenon of social roles devoid of content, the gap between social and biological death, the tension between meaning and control, the incongruence between social image and self-image, and the replacement of linear time by cyclical time all suggest that structural relations among phenomena are more significant than the phenomena in themselves.[3] We began by observing that ageing is conceived as a problem for society, and it was argued that the real problem is neither the allocation of resources nor the genuine or feigned functional disabilities of the aged but identity and the meaning of life, not for the aged but for those around them. These fundamental questions are generated by the disruption and disorder in the social field and cognitive map that constitute the world view of the non-aged and, indirectly, of the aged too. The disorientation and confusion surrounding the aged emerge not from their designation as a distinct symbolic category but from the ambiguity inherent in their position at the brink of the unknown – their function as a buffer between life and death.

Thus the cultural enclave constructed for the elderly resembles the liminal stage of a rite of passage. As are initiates, the old are stripped of their roles and symbolic trappings and excluded from the category of full human beings. Stigmatization and labelling ensure the imposition on them of a false homogeneity, and the humiliation and degradation they experience reinforce the analogy. In view of the absence of a socially defined destination for this transformative process, however, the parallel between the aged and initiates undergoing a rite of passage cannot be sustained. Rather, a state of limbo becomes permanent, and transition is superseded by stagnation. Furthermore, while sometimes the blurring of category boundaries receives social legitimation, ageing remains associated with the untouchable and abominable. The mixing and trans-formation of symbolic worlds in the circus – the transmutation of sexual attributes, size and age, and animality and humanity – are part of one's childhood lessons (see Bouissac 1976), and reversal of roles, statuses, and moral standards lies at the heart of play, drama and ritual. Ageing, however, is out of bounds, associated with demonic power. Thus, the country of the old is a no-man's-land devoid of the educational messages embedded in other dissolved cultural categories. In contrast to the stranger,[4] who may serve to represent the socially undesirable, the aged disguised as a social problem, remain ill-defined.

Charged with ambiguities and inconsistencies that make its cultural decipherment almost impossible, old age is enigmatic at all levels of consciousness and occupies unexplorable social territory. The power of stereotypes rests in their capacity to obfuscate and yet circumscribe such territory. Through stereotypes the dualism of purity and danger (see Douglas 1966; Steiner 1956) inherent in the cultural position of the old is managed in a socially acceptable manner, thus enabling the non-aged to treat the old as both victims and demonic forces. To describe old age in our society in this fashion is not to deny the concrete problems related to ageing or the enormous diversity within the social category of the aged. It is, however, to suggest that it is the socio-cultural act of definition that informs these realities. That the aged are segregated, constrained and transformed into dependent human beings is not the consequence of objective difficulties in functioning but the result of fundamental dilemmas concerning the perception of the aged and the acquisition of knowledge about them.

The cultural-symbolic space occupied by the old is therefore to be understood as a refracted reflection of some of the key issues of human existence. In this space time stops, body is separated from mind, and life meets death. It offers no direction or orientation but only constant perplexity as to the nature of the world and its order. It is a futureless universe in which resources do not aggregate towards any goal. Since the organization of resources in the reality of the aged is governed by its own rules, the structure of interpersonal relationships among them can be expected to be qualitatively different from that of relationships among the non-aged. In other words, the argument that the aged occupy a unique cultural-symbolic space should be corroborated by the way in which the aged construct their world. We have already seen some examples of this construction. Examination of the relationship between the boundaries separating the aged from the rest of society and the internal boundaries among the aged themselves may lead to an understanding of the aged that does not require ill-founded assumptions about their inner world.

The boundaries between the aged and their socio-cultural environment are neither territorial nor personal but conceptual. The separation is confirmed and reinforced by a range of symbolic expressions among which advocacy of 'integration' of the aged into society is prominent. Separate and restricted, the aged are free to construct a social world appropriate to their situation. The pre-conditions for this endeavor include abandonment of aspirations to mobility, recognition of the inability to match control to meaning, and pursuit of self-knowledge rather than acceptance of imposed images. If these preconditions are met, then age-homogeneous communities characterized by rejection of the outside world, the dissolution of internal boundaries among the participants, and the creation of a new alignment between the desirable and the attainable may emerge. Underlying this proposition is the assumption that the ultimate objective of the aged is to arrest the change that spells deterioration and inevitable death. This objective may be accomplished by redesigning social space and thus eliminating the competition and hierarchy that generate social dynamics, disregarding the non-aged, denying death, eschewing intimate relationships (since these are liable to be terminated), and constantly repeating the same behavioural patterns as if time could be dissected into self-contained units. The messages conveyed through such channels of communication, informed neither by the past nor by plans for the future, are likely to be either strictly instrumental or surrealistic. In other words, control is either entirely separated from meaning or completely congruent with it. In the latter instance there is a complete breakdown of temporal boundaries.[5]

Ageing as an existential state is not amenable to conventional sociological explanations, and to the extent to which support systems for the aged are informed by academic constructs they are misguided. If the caregiver's image of the old does not reflect the experience of being old, then the services rendered, rather than providing relief and well-being, may serve only to induce further frustration and degradation. If ageing is to be understood, an analytic model suited to it must be developed (see Fabian 1983). The assumptions guiding the prevailing approach to the understanding of ageing are inadequate, the concept of self attributed to the elderly is irrelevant, and the terms of reference within which the existential world of the elderly is understood are inappropriate.

The study of ageing assumes that ageing is primarily a natural phenomenon whose course, notwithstanding its socio-cultural and psychological concomitants, is predetermined, that it is a reflection of the existential conditions of the category of individuals labelled 'old', and that it is a process explicable in linear, dynamic terms. The validity of all of these assumptions can be contested. The first is challenged by the cultural diversity of ageing in different societies and in various contexts (though, of course, biological-physiological determinants are not to be dismissed). Beliefs, images, and attitudes regarding ageing vary with socio-cultural conditions. The second renders old age different to other stages of the life course or cycle, in which social space is defined by hierarchical order, mobility, and a system of exchange. The third is called into question by the evidence discussed earlier that for the aged time has no cumulative, progressive meaning.

Because most old people continue to live in multi-generational milieu, their inverted conceptions of time are enmeshed in an unyielding reality premised on their opposites. The situation generates a split between inner experience and outward appearances (see Cohen and Eisdorfer 1986; Eckert 1980; Neugarten 1977). Since the provision of the needs of the old largely depends on their 'adaptation' to environmental expectations, their behavioural patterns are designed to elicit the most resources at the least cost, and this means divorcing the inner self from the outer self, 'I' from 'me' (Mead 1934; Zimring 1988), behaviour from personality, and person from persona.

Living this way requires a great deal of determination and energy. The outer self continues to act and interact in the linear, culturally acceptable manner expected and rewarded by the social environment. Symbolically sustained by social responses, behaviour in the social world consists of messages connecting meaning to control, ends to means, self to context. Here 'adjustment' takes the form of rational utilization and mobilization of available resources. Various means are sought, tested, and employed to muster services, social support and personal assets in an effort to maintain an acceptable level of well-being. The inner self, however, functions differently. Symbolic structures create an atemporal universe of meaning consisting of significant memories, tokens of cherished identity, and freely constructed life materials. This mental edifice is capable of accommodating infinite plausible self-images whose very existence serves as their justification. As a self-sufficient, insular system, it has mythlike properties, combining elements of personal genesis, the presentation and resolution of fundamental questions of meaning, and orientation in social space and time. Narratives in the form of reminiscences and life review may bear witness to such internal processes.

The split between the inner self, consisting of a pool of culturally acquired codes and categorizations, and the outer self, embedded in the structure of social control, would seem to suggest schism between culture and society. Most studies of old age focus on the outer self, only a few venturing beyond appearances to examine the practices of life review and reminiscence and even fewer attempting to straddle the two. It is telling that the one behavioural arena in which culture and society – 'the dreamt of' and 'the lived in' – are likely to converge, ritual, has not received scholarly treatment by gerontologists. The scant socio-anthropological evidence of ritual among the aged in Western society may well attest to its relative scarcity, suggesting in turn that inner and outer selves do not meet in their daily lives and thereby corroborating my proposal of a barrier between them. The participation of elders in ceremonial activities in simple societies further supports the contention, since it suggests that when elderly persons are full-fledged members of society there is no need for a self-contrived division between inner and outer selves.

The distinction between the two modes of constituting experience may be viewed as a distinction between a symbolic and a mythical orientation, between contextual analysis and textual explanation, between selfless age and 'ageless self' (Kaufman 1986), or, once again, between control and meaning. It is part of the fabric of modern life, in which fragmentation, compartmentalization, and symbolic differentiation prevail. The 'homeless mind' is forever wandering from one domain of identity to another, the divided self a reflection of incoherent and diverse life-worlds (see Berger, Berger and Kellner 1973; Schutz and Luckmann 1973). The condition of the elderly in our society compels them at times to exaggerate this duality of matter and mind, body and spirit, the existentialist and the existential.

The structural condition of being old in modern society denies the elderly a firm anchor in their socio-cultural universe. As 'disengaged', 'symbolically invisible', and 'roleless', they float in a social vacuum within which the disparate fragments of the self are not subject to any significant unifying force. This state, in part attributable to the lack of socialization to old age (Rosow 1974), lends itself to an infinite range of arrangements and rearrangements of experience, most of which remain unreported. Evidence for this may perhaps be found in the repetitive utterances of the elderly, arguably the consequence of a non-cumulative idea of time sequence in which one temporal unit no longer feeds the subsequent one so as to build up a sense of duration (see Luscher 1974). Apparent loss of memory may perhaps be interpreted as an attempt to return to the safe haven of a past universe of meaning. Belligerent, cantankerous behaviour may suggest an awareness of the aged's 'nothing to lose' situation, while sudden, extreme shifts in behaviour may accurately reflect the fractured existential world in which the elderly live. Above all, the establishment of boundaries between the old and the non-old by and for the old, as in old-age-homogeneous communities, may serve as testimony to the notion that meaningful communication with the old can only take place among the old. Since the aged live in a zero-sum-game situation of limited gains and dwindling resources, their capacity to draw upon their environment to enrich their inner experience is relatively restricted. Whereas imagination, fantasy, rationalization and reconstruction may allow any material to be processed in the construction of a viable self, it is reasonable to presume that old, cherished experiences, entirely amenable to manipulation, will outweigh new and mostly unfavourable ones in eligibility for admission into the guarded core of positive identity.

Since this 'adjustment' is non-developmental (McCulloch 1980) and non-diachronic, it may well stand in contradiction to the Eriksonian model. Structural, synchronic, and 'ecological', it is perhaps more amenable to anthropological than to psychological inquiry. The contours of 'experience' – reported or attributed – are established not in terms of the self but in terms of the relationship among its often diverse manifestations. The holistic nature of anthropological inquiry may allow the student of ageing some measure of access to the frame within which such experience is shaped. However, since that frame is fragmented, the so-called phenomenon of ageing is only partly understandable through observation.

Time, space and self are fuzzy concepts, but the following ethnographic description may offer some evidence for a number of the notions just discussed. While the case presented is by no means representative of all age-homogeneous settings or an argument for the benefit of such settings, it does reveal the code and content of time, space, and meaning peculiar to the aged. The creation in this case of a mirror image of the world of the non-aged demonstrates the transformation of the past into a diametrically opposed present. This dichotomy draws on the split between the two selves – the social-existential and the personal-existentialist.

The population under study consisted of about four hundred members of a day centre for elderly Jewish residents of London's East End, one of the city's poorest neighbourhoods. As first-generation descendants of East European immigrant Jews, members of the centre were characterized by poverty, illiteracy, and alienation both from their better-off Jewish peers and from the non-Jewish working-class residents of the East End, who regarded them as an economic threat. After the devastation of the East End during World War II, much of the more affluent Jewish population of the area had moved to other parts of London. In addition, many of the younger generation had also migrated to better parts of the metropolis, leaving behind an ageing population suffering from a lack of community life, lowered standards of living, and social isolation. Inability to travel and ill health aggravated their situation, and the fact that their low incomes had to be supplemented by charitable organizations subjected them to further loss of dignity and independence.

The changes in members' existential conditions were not anchored in a corresponding set of social definitions. Their severance from their social environments engendered disenchantment and a growing discrepancy between the perceived values of the non-aged society and the meaning they themselves attributed to their lives. The gap between social conceptions and personal plight and the resulting awareness of the arbitrariness and inadequacy of former associations and commitments facilitated the creation of an alternative reality, the main constituent of which was the reconstruction of the temporal universe.

The relative importance of future and past in members' lives was apparent from their conversations. Three principles guided selections made from their past lives: (1) Nostalgic recollections from early childhood years, given pride of place, were elaborated upon and richly embellished. (2) Socio-economic and occupational histories were obliterated altogether. (3) Events such as participation in anti-Fascist demonstrations during the 1930s and hospitalization, among others, were highly valued and respected. Application of these principles created a shared egalitarianism and social immobility in both structure and content, thus placing the revised past on a continuum with the present. The future was handled by avoidance. The possibility of being placed in an old-age home or a geriatric ward was dismissed out of hand. Members often renounced their families and instead referred to one another as 'brothers' and 'sisters'. Everything was geared towards the present, and thus when death occurred it was ignored. Members were totally committed to the ideology that a meaningful life was based on principles of boundless care and unconditional help. When talking about the distant past, members often implied that, in contrast to the current situation in the outside world, their early relationships had been dominated by mutual aid and community care. Any gesture of help from the outside was invariably interpreted as a humiliating act rendering the recipients 'non-human'.

The guiding ideology of the centre was help and care; if one was willing to help and was in need of help oneself, then one was eligible for admission into the centre milieu. A sense of belonging to the centre could be gained only by full immersion in the care system. Inside the centre neither 'favours' nor 'rewards' had any place. The giving of care constituted the sole criterion for esteem, and the right to give and receive help was unconditional. The importance of this moral code to the perspective on time rests in the structure of its practices rather than in its content. In the centre, the unconditional acts of giving and taking were independent of each other; no act instituted any indebtedness on the part of donor or recipient. This allowed the establishment of a present-bound society. This liminal framework or 'limbo time', together with the suppression of creativity and denial of personal achievement, generated an environment immune to change.

The question arises of whether this arresting of time was in fact a sort of play. Play involves the separation of means from ends (Miller 1973) and the merging of subject and object in atemporality (Handelman 1990). Notwithstanding its importance, it seems that here what we as outsiders might perceive as 'play' is in fact the subjective reality of the participants. The elderly never asserted, 'this is play', the metacommunicational signal that is necessary for identification of behaviour as play (Bateson 1972: 177–94). However, the question remains open.

Conclusions: the nature of knowledge about ageing

The separation of selves makes any attempt to address the issue of old age in a given context extremely problematic. The shifting involvements of elderly people are often tacit, and this makes the seemingly tried-and-true concept of context inappropriate to their study. Knowledge about old age must therefore be produced in ways different to conventional socio-anthropological ones. Knowledge and ignorance are socially constructed, and the scope and nature of available knowledge are culturally determined. Knowledge is produced and reproduced by weaving selected units of information into models of interpretation and modes of thinking. The key to this process is discovering the basic assumptions about the world, fundamental beliefs, and root metaphors by which human perception is shaped.

The languages of ageing described in this book are different aspects of a single metalanguage – the dialectics of culture and society. Because context is uninformative here, however, any attempt to develop a vocabulary appropriate to and emerging from the generative grammar of ageing is doomed to failure. Acontextual constructs are rare in socio-anthropological discourse, and those referred to in the course of this book – for example, the symbolic type – do not appear to be adequate to the task of explaining old age. Alternatives to a context-bound perspective might include an approach that sees communication between the old and their human environment as taking place through core cultural codes rather than interaction (Lévi-Strauss 1967; Unruh 1983). These 'social worlds' create foci of shared interest without entailing a necessary commitment to face-to-face relationships and may enable people to accommodate their identities to selectively available universes of images and meanings. Another such acontextual approach might be through the notion of liminality. Originating, as we have seen, in the study of rites of passage, the atemporal, anti-structural state of being socially disengaged and culturally unemcumbered, might be appropriate for describing the situation of the aged. All these possibilities, however, only further obscure the issue. The antithetical language of 'disengagement', 'liminality', and 'disintegration' attests to impasse.

As Strathern (1987) has described it, the notion of context in social anthropology is a reflection of a holistic perspective on society. A post-modern orientation to the understanding of social phenomena would replace this notion with the idea of diverse texts produced by various cultural agents. The approach to the aged being advocated here is consistent with this orientation. Elderly people generate different texts of identity (Shotter and Gergen 1988), the incoherence of which is reflected in the phenomenon of old age. The three concepts suggested above – symbolic types, social worlds, and liminality – represent three texts in which ageing is addressed. Furthermore, the notion of a split between inner and outer self alludes to the idea of a 'double personality' (Lifton 1983, 1986). Since the conception of old age involves myriad languages, it is linguistic phenomena that must replace context as the focus for its anthropological study. Borrowing the concept of 'intertextuality' (Kristeva 1980), our discussion addresses the inconsistent texts of ageing on the assumption that examining the interconnections of these texts will produce knowledge otherwise inaccessible.

Clearly, it is context and practical systems of accountability that allow humans to formulate symbolic classifications and cultural themes. Thus the construction of social knowledge is contextually conditioned. It follows therefore that the understanding of ageing must be culturally relative and socially diverse. However, the universe of knowledge out of which the imagery of ageing and the aged emerges is at once overcontextualized and undercontextualized. It is overcontextualized in that the condition of the aged is attributed to the circumstances of daily living and the availability of socio-political and economic resources. It is undercontextualized in that the cultural category of the aged is considered dominated by universal concerns such as the boundary between life and death. The conception of the aged as a symbolic type attests to this latter condition. Simultaneously context-bound and out-of-context, our society's various narratives on ageing are manifest in policy-making documents, social workers' reports, newspaper articles, fiction, ethnographic accounts, and, indeed, theoretical paradigms.

Deciphering such accounts involves the recognition of two contrasting codes, socio-cultural and existential. While the former captures the elderly as 'ordinary people', the latter projects some of the key dilemmas of being human onto the construct of the 'old', and the separation of the two renders any reference to ageing multivocal. The shifting attention to different voices about ageing reflects changes in the self-awareness of the auditor – from socially conscious participant or commentator to observer of the essence of human nature. Attitudes towards ageing may thus serve as indicators of choices made between alternative, sometimes competing, models of reality. In one sense, the choice is between an interest in human diversity, and a concern with human universals. In another sense, it could be regarded as a stand taken in the perennial debate between pragmatism and idealism, practical reasoning and metaphysical preoccupation. Cultural texts concerning ageing are therefore also testimonials to the predispositions and outlooks of their producers. This last is of particular importance in the case of knowledge of old age, since the authorship of ageing-related texts often implies authority. The cultural positioning of the old may have implications for the exercise of social control, the distribution of power, and the allocation of resources. Thus the decoding of such texts may serve to throw hidden paradigms into sharp relief.

These two codes originate in ambivalence on the part of the non-aged – their fear of death and their desire for intergenerational continuity. Therefore the social construction of ageing must be viewed as brinkmanship, and this has implications for the world of the elderly. Old age is best understood as a form of post-modern existence in which the mobilization of meaning is fluid and constant and confrontation with the self is continuous. The only appropriate explanatory model of ageing draws on our thus far limited knowledge of the relations among the factors that shape it (see, e.g.,

Birren and Bengston 1988; Cole and Gradow 1986; Keith et al. 1986; Reinharz and Rowles 1988; Woodward and Schwarz 1988; Porter and Porter 1984). Our eclipsed view of ageing may be a form of defence against death, but it may also invoke associations from the ill-defined domains of the occult, fantasy and imagination and draw upon the worlds of the handicapped, the terminally and chronically sick, the stranger, the adolescent and the unemployed. Hence analogy, deconstruction and possibly reconstruction are the only methods available for its comprehension. Reconstructing texts on ageing in terms of 'social problems', 'social structure', and 'cultural values' is, however, bound to misrepresent the phenomenon and misguide the concerned social agent. It is in the interstices of our various approaches to ageing that its true nature may be captured. A systematically analytic perspective will have to resort to non-poetic, non-literate devices which, though inadequate to convey the sense and experience of being human, will nevertheless protect us against the unfathomable and the ambiguous. Such 'ideal language' ought to be sought in forms of notation where one name denotes one thing. As Gellner (1973:159) remarks, this kinky achievement is an 'attaining of what philosophers who wanted an ideal language had hoped for: namely that logically necessary relationships should be "shown", be evident, from the very notation, so that only synthetic, factual truths need actually be asserted'. In the case of referring to old age, that would mean a systematic endeavour to demystify and demetaphorize the semantic zone of describing and analysing it. Stark events and facts, signs rather than symbols, self-contained circles rather than open-ended linear pathways. Recoursing to such modes of articulating ageing stands in sharp opposition to the customary fashion by which social knowledge of old age is shaped. Concepts of pejorative change, deterioration, maladjustment and incompetence constitute the main vocabulary of this social model.

Knowledge of ageing, then, is a type of masking – often simply an academically celebrated form of necessary social ignorance. Whereas the endless pursuit of knowledge about ageing endows the phenomenon with the illusion of intelligibility, that very quest renders it unique and inexplicable. Hence the production of know-ledge about ageing is self-subversive. In this sense, this book is yet another example of the potency of knowledge about ageing as a social construct and the impossibility of pursuing it as an intellectual enterprise.

The inaccessibility of the experience of being old, coupled with the inadequacy of available conceptual frameworks, calls for an entirely different kind of approach to the acquisition of knowledge about ageing. The horizons of our understanding might be broadened if such knowledge were treated as a new form of discourse, an 'episteme' of another human sphere,[1] informed by our knowledge of the structure of human universals and comprised of information that is non-conceptual, non-verbal. It is such discourse that might eventually replace academic conventions, social lip-service and personal bigotry. Knowledge of ageing could thus be constructed and applied as a test case to our own self-knowledge at any age. The importance of gerontology is not in its substantive contribution to the understanding of the nature of old age but in its allusion to the limits of our knowledge of the essence of human existence. The main instructive value of seeking knowledge of ageing is the potential it offers for facilitating an untried and vanguard experiment in unlearning and debunking.

The argument of this book has involved a number of self-subversive attempts to gain knowledge about old age. These divergent models all fail to recognize what is fundamental to the phenomenon in question – the puzzling and compelling schism that emanates from the perennial division between life and death and generates other separations such as 'society' and 'the aged', 'culture' and 'society', and 'inner self' and 'outer self' or 'existentialist' and 'existential'. The quest for knowledge about old age must therefore take account of its divided imagery. Scholars endeavouring to enunciate the socio-cultural dimension of ageing (Butler 1975; de Beauvoir 1975) have intermingled social concepts of old age with the presumed experience of older people. Underlying these models is the assumption of a nexus between 'us' and 'them': 'Fundamental to the study of symbolic anthropology is the concern with how people formulate their reality. We must, if we are to understand this and relate it to an understanding of their (and our own) action, examine *their* culture not *our theories* and if we study our theories we must study them as "their culture", study them as a system of

94

symbols not our *ad hoc* presumptions about what it might or should be' (Dolgin, Demnitzer and Schneider 1977: 34). Many studies, however, reaching an impasse, give voice to doubts concerning the very possibility of eliciting a coherent image of old age. Such doubts are manifest, for instance, in the observation that the non-old and the old are unable to communicate with each other. 'The aged do appear strange to those integrated into the societal mainstream, however, the dominant cultural beliefs and practices that characterize mainstream are themselves hardly familiar to those who have long since stopped swimming in those fast-moving waters' (Dowd 1986: 155). The split between the 'mainstream' and the world of the aged 'stranger' engenders a cosmology of symbolic types – in the form of wise men, saints, and witches (Turnbull 1984: 223–62) in simple societies or their modern demonic counterparts, the 'scheming hag' and the 'dear old thing' (Cool and McCabe 1983: 56–71). However, the theoretical implications of the split image of the old have rarely been taken into consideration. The observation by Lifton (1983; 1986) that personality may take two divergent, even separate forms gives a new complexion to the production of old-age related knowledge. If this observation is correct then old age must be addressed in terms of the ambivalent nature of inner and outer experiences as manifest in the behaviour of the elderly within their social milieu.

The implications of this split image for the social character of old age are far-reaching. To begin with, it is clear that sociological analyses do not inform social conditions. Furthermore, since a monolithic perception of the ageing individual is invalid, communication with the elderly based on conceptions of the aged 'personality' and 'self' may be misguided. Finally, issues of bioethics such as euthanasia and social support must withstand the scrutiny of the dual representation of old age, abandoning the idea of 'managing the aged' and the identification of old people with old age. The translation of these principles into social action would require both overcoming the consequences of the ageism that is so prevalent in modern society (see Phillipson 1982) and conceiving of the members of any category of people, and particularly the 'roleless' and the stigmatized, as having multiple identities to choose from. Emphasizing disunity rather than unity, fragmentation rather than cohesion, and incongruity rather than consistency might facilitate the production of knowledge about ageing which does not imply cultural exclusion.

In this regard the analysis of the ageing self draws on other studies that have focused on the question of the authenticity of the self as opposed to its flexibility and adaptability to social constraints. The issue is evident, for example, in studies emphasizing the notion of 'the double bind of the separative self of women' whose authentic identity is denied by their accountability to men (Bonds 1990). It is also proposed as one of the crucial features of modern society as manifested in contemporary American life (Bellah et al. 1985). Thus, our own discourse of ageing is neither acultural nor specific but rather presents a case in point by which we may rid ourselves of some of our cultural preconceptions regarding the nature of self-hood, relationships and social order.

Such unleashing may suggest a post-modern view of ageing and, indeed, as some scholars claim (Featherstone and Hepworth 1991), the experience of old age straddles multiple life worlds. Using Giddens's metaphor for post-modernism as a form of social nomadism between unconnected places (Giddens 1991), Bauman maintains that, unlike a pilgrim who plans his journey to a destination of worship, nomads, 'if pressed to make sense of their itinerary would rather look back than forward tracing (with the "wisdom of hindsight") the connections between stations which they failed to note at the time ... only in this *ex post facto* sense would they speak of their lives as of implementation of a life project' (Bauman 1992: 167).

The language of the old studied in this book reflects that observation of separate narratives post-factually unified. However, the language about the old – that of representations – is of a different nature; it implies a foretold master-narrative of striving for immortality and denial of death (Lifton 1977; Bauman 1992). This life project of modern man has old age as its protagonist. Against the grain of multiculturalism and pastiche reality stands the ultimate and absolute certainty of death, whose imminence can be forestalled by the penultimate phase of life – old age. Thus at the midst of contemporary western post-modern experience, old age reveals itself as a vestige of linearity and modernity. The following ethnographic reflection shows how the two modes of articulating life narratives – the modern and the post-modern – intermingle to form a symbolic blend of media representation of old age as heralding death alongside its presentation by the old as a pool of diverse cultural choices. Knowledge of old age should, in terms of this book, emerge in the interstices between the two.

ETHNOGRAPHIC REFLECTION: THE AGED AS A SYMBOLIC TYPE

Plath (1980), who has studied the relationship between literature and ageing in modern Japan, maintains that individual biographies merge in collective history, thus creating a sense of cumulative duration. This perspective suggests that there is an uninterrupted, mutually reinforcing flow of information between the various sections of the 'portfolio of the self'. In a society where knowledge of ageing is subject to mutually exclusive acquisitions by the old and the non-old, no such unified, coherent narrative is attainable. The first of the case studies that follow presents the aged as a symbolic type which, while purporting to represent the experience of being old, is in fact only tenuously linked to that experience. The second is a response by the aged to this kind of imagery – a research paper on television representations of the old. Here the experience-near conception is validated in terms of experience-distant references. The observer becomes the observed and the object of knowledge and its subject are indivisible.

In 1986 Israeli television and radio dedicated an entire day of nationwide broadcasting to the plight of the elderly in Israel. The highlight of this event was a seven-hour television show entitled 'Teletrom for the Old', which, using documentary film, interviews, and appeals by leading public figures and top entertainers, solicited monetary contributions to be distributed among various organizations caring for the old. The symbolic type of the aged constructed in the course of the broadcast consisted of four stages from victim to social sacrifice, with one stage emerging from the previous one and heralding its successor. A parallel was drawn between the aged as a category and as the members of such a category to describing the aged as '10 per cent of the population who are lonely, vulnerable, and destitute' – a description that not only ignored the facts of Israeli society but also failed to recognize any heterogeneity among those depicted. The general term 'the old' was used to articulate the condition of all old people: 'Imagine the old lonely person living in a cramped flat without furniture and with no conveniences'. The inevitable dependency on society involved here was stressed throughout the broadcast. Another aspect of this dependency was vulnerability to physical assault, the old person being depicted as a defenceless potential victim. The aged were portrayed as incapable of self-help and their problem as fundamentally insoluble. The question raised at this stage, to be resolved in the next, was why the aged were a perennial problem.

The 'answer' to this question, presented in the second stage of the broadcast, was that the old were a product of natural (i.e., physio-biological) processes. Here the medicalization of ageing contributed to the projection of an image of the old as conditioned by determi-nistic objective factors. Thus, reports from geriatric wards and nursing homes were accompanied by interviews with elderly persons involving questions such as 'When did age first hit you?', the interviewer implying that nature must despise the old to treat them the way it does. The old were presented as the product of inevitable pathological changes, unrelated to any social context and therefore subject to no moral order or system of accountability. This image of them – their humanity rendered doubtful – served to justify their alienation from society. The highlight of this stage was a report on the performance by an old-age pensioner's club of Moliére's *The Hypochondriac*, represented by both actors and presenter as a show of self-derision based on the insignificance of real or feigned disease in the face of incurable old age. Here old was closely linked with foolish, and the question was raised of whether the aged deserved social support. The answer was that since they were the product of a neutral force (i.e., nature), keeping them within society was divinely ordained. The reasons for and the meaning of the strangeness of the old and their estrangement from society remained to be considered in the third stage.

Although death was never mentioned, it permeated the broad-cast. The implied association between death and the old posed a dilemma for viewers: while they might be tempted to dissociate the old from the human context, they could not do so because, as one of the presenters said, 'We are all going to be old one day'. Rejection of the old in the form of territorial sequestration or social isolation was impossible because of their physical visibility. Reluctant awareness of these reminders of one's finitude was expressed by one presenter: 'Behold, they are among us, we cannot ignore them, we must help them'. This last plea for collective help constituted the 'answer' to the third question and led to the final stage of the construction of the old as a symbolic type.

Helping the aged, the main overt justification for the show, also constituted its contextual core. Well-known personalities appealed to the public to offer financial or material assistance. Thus, public organizations, commercial companies, etc., tried to outdo each other while at the same time submerging themselves in what was declared a communal commitment. One factor, however, was noticeably absent, namely, any suggestion of personal care, family support or community obligation towards the elderly. Personal accountability was thus dissolved into collective responsibility, whose moral burden was to be discharged through the success of the show. Since collective guilt was the latent message communicated by the broadcast (an example of this was an appeal made by the president of Israel urging all citizens to make amends), the old became the mechanism through which moral absolution was to be achieved. The motif of the altruistic gift furnished the construct of the old with the unilateral relationship that rendered it an object. Once reified, this object could not only serve as a communal sacrifice on the altar of collective ambivalence towards the aged, but also achieve autonomy beyond context and setting. Legitimated by the state, the broadcast epitomized and confirmed cultural dilemmas concerning the symbolic states of the old apart from any particular social context. The distance between performers and spectators was conducive to maintaining the boundary between everyday life, with its familiar elderly, and the play-cum-ritual construction of the old as a symbolic type.

While the case study of the day centre was framed by the idea of liminality and the technography of the image of the old in the mass media by the construct of the symbolic type, one further case study illustrates the creation of a social world – an extended web of meanings and actions centred around one symbolic focus of interest. The study concerns elderly people whose common ground was their involvement in a self-help organization, the University of the Third Age in Cambridge, England. The university was a voluntary association with a membership of about five hundred engaged in a variety of learning and social activities. It organized study groups on a wide range of subjects, initiated a host of cultural events, and promoted social links among its members. Although admission into the university was not deliberately selective, most members were highly literate and socially and economically well established, being primarily retired professionals and academics.

Knowledge, as the main objective of the organization, was not only disseminated, circulated, and exchanged but also produced by its members. Through its active research committee and in the course of social gatherings and formal study, concepts, perspectives, and approaches underwent revision, reassessment, and remoulding. It was not so much new information that was accrued as novel cognitive patterns and modes of experience. Basic to this experience was the construction of devices for dismantling lifelong beliefs and principles whose relevance to the members' current lives was no longer certain. In other words, members were learning to 'unlearn'. Evidence of this 'unlearning' was manifest in a variety of activities to which members brought the potent research tool of reflexivity.

One might have expected this reflexivity to lead to the use of personal histories as mirroring devices for present existence, but the idea of tape-recording their life histories received no support, and neither did the idea of reconstructing the local heritage through members' autobiographical accounts. A complex research project on funeral arrangements in Cambridge was abandoned when members were confronted with questions concerning attitudes towards death, and another study on old-age homes was aborted. Most intriguing, the exchange of views in a classroom situation revealed unexpected attitudes towards knowledge. Reading was dismissed as superfluous if not misleading. Mediated accounts of reality were viewed as 'unnatural' and 'distorting' in comparison with direct personal experience. Members insisted on engaging in discourse on what they called 'life itself', a dispassionate examination of events and views on general existential issues. Family life, for example, was discussed not in the context of intergenerational relationships but rather in terms of universal human dilemmas such as freedom and identity versus duty. Debates on human nature and the values that should guide it drew on both current events and history, prehistory, and myth. Other cognitive strategies for reconstituting reality included avoidance of intimacy, renunciation of love, criticism of the British socio-political system, and contempt for status symbols, especially those conferred on academics and doctors. As one member put it, 'We must take it from first principles' and 'see life with a third-age eye'.

According to the foreword to the university's research report *The Image of the Elderly on T.V.*,

> On 21st July 1981, in the Guildhall at Cambridge, we adopted the word 'University' at the first meeting of what was to become The University of the Third Age, because it seemed the proper description of our intentions. From the outset, however, we have recognized that we could defend this title only if our institution did what it could to add to knowledge, as universities do. By this we meant knowledge in general, of any kind, such knowledge as with our resources we could recover or help to recover. The knowledge we are particularly after, however, is knowledge of ourselves, as those in the Third Age, of our place in the society to which we belong, and of the situation of that society as a whole in respect of age, ageing and ageism. We want to be as helpful as we can to those in the Third Age, in intellectual and practical matters too.
>
> The Research Committee of the University of the Third Age in Cambridge has existed therefore since March 1982, when people were first enrolled in an exercise demonstrating what a University of the Third Age might be able to do, held at St. John's College, Cambridge. The original members of that original committee even did some research, on the spot, by going into the Cambridge market place one afternoon and asking people they met whether it was possible for the elderly to learn something new. The answers were overwhelmingly affirmative.
>
> The present report is, as will be seen, the first of what we hope will be a series and does fit, we believe, the description set out above. The Research Committee is already engaged on a second project.

The kind of knowledge sought and pursued by members of the University of the Third Age was 'new' in the sense that it was not imposed on them by others and was therefore deemed authentic and unmediated. Recognizing their own limitations both as researchers and as elderly persons, the authors of the report concluded, contrary to countless research reports (Harris and Feinberg 1978), that the image they were investigating was 'fair':

> On Channel 4 one of the two advertisements showing the elderly was: Go Smash an Egg! in which Barbara Woodhouse appeared. Five monitors happen to have commented on this advertisement. Three considered that it presented a fair image of the woman in her 70s as 'active, fit, content, neat'. 'Came over as a figure of authority, fairly pleasantly'. The other two rated this advertisement as presenting an unfair image: 'Very silly advertisement – quite ridiculous', 'Given silly comments; did not seem at ease with her words and gestures'. These circumstances can be taken as evidence of how different reactions can be, an overriding difficulty of research of this kind. A Road Safety advertisement showed a Chelsea pensioner helping an elderly woman across a road. One monitor commented that 'a romantic meeting was suggested as a reward for observing the Code. Humorous, but the old were presented as vulnerable – which, of course, they are at Zebra crossings. 'Faintly undignified'. The commentator announced 'You are only old once'.

Having satisfied themselves that their findings were objective and credible, they went on to conclude:

> Contrary to the generally accepted impression, based mainly on US research, that TV programmes denigrate the elderly and propagate unfavourable stereotypes, British TV (BBC and ITV) present the elderly fairly, even in fictional programming. While few advertisements portray older people, when they are presented they are shown in a fair and sympathetic way. However, although they are usually justly treated, the elderly appear on British television far less often than is justified by their proportion of the population and their importance in people's experience. Perhaps their non-appearance betrays stereotypical attitudes on the part of television producers who judge the elderly to be marginal, boring and of little account. If this is the case, we might usefully ask how far this actually reflects the attitudes of audiences towards the elderly. There is evidence, however, that in thinking of old people in real life, the public in general affirm the positive attitudes of the elderly and reject the negative. (IBA, Television and the Elderly, 1980)

Notes

Introduction: towards knowledge of old age

1 Rather than adopting the phenomenological approach of McKee (1982), Philibert (1982), or Fontana (1976), I consider Rosow's (1974) perspective closest to my own. Clark and Anderson's (1967) study of the relationship between culture and ageing and Riley, Johnson and Foner's (1972) seminal research on ageing and society were also invaluable models. Gubrium's (1986) work can certainly be seen as an important contribution from this perspective.

2 Without attempting to enter into a discourse regarding the nature of knowledge, I would point out at the outset that a distinction must be made between 'understanding' and 'explanation'. Following Taylor's (1985) analysis of Ricoeur's philosophy, I use the former to indicate the key myths and images that frame our perception of the world and the latter to address the logical rational edifice that follows that core trope. Clearly, while understanding is not amenable to refutation, explanation is open to critical scrutiny in its own terms.

1 The social trap: the language of separation

1 The association between human categories and classification and linguistic structures is deeply entrenched in socio-anthropological thought and is borne out in numerous theoretical forms. Inspired by Douglas's perspective on the connection between cultural classification and social control (Douglas 1966; 1970; 1978), Bernstein's work on the correlation between linguistic codes and social structures (Bernstein 1971; 1972; 1973) and by Goody's arguments concerning the role of literacy in literate society (Goody 1979), gerontological literature has directly or indirectly drawn on some of these notions in endeavouring to propose a set of attributes of the aged person (see, e.g., Kaufman 1986; Dowd 1980, 1986).

103

2 On the complex issue of the interrelationship between culture and personality, see Shweder and Levine (1984). The position taken here is evidently that so-called personality is a social construct, a reification of cultural properties.
3 Of the vast literature on stigma, Goffman's (1963) outstanding contribution should be mentioned. Butler's (1969, 1975) work on the stigmatization of the aged and the resulting 'ageism' is an application of this perspective. The term 'human obsolescence', coined by J. Henry (1963), points to the social consequences of this process.
4 A short list of current scientific periodicals on the subject includes the *International Journal of Aging and Human Development*, the *Journal of Gerontology*, the *Journal of Aging Studies, Research on Aging, Comprehensive Aging, The Gerontologist, Aging and Society*, and the *Journal of Cross-Cultural Gerontology*. For a comprehensive reference on the social aspects of ageing, see Binstock and Shanas (1976, 1985).
5 Ever since Bismarck introduced retirement as one of his welfare measures, age has had legal features which have generated solid social facts (on the implications of this, see Cain 1974). The historical question of the beginning of 'old age' in English culture is discussed by Roebuck (1976).
6 The distinction between a social problem and a sociological issue is essential to our discussion; while the former is beyond its scope, the latter is at its core (see Berger 1966).
7 Conceivably Martin Buber's (1973) concept of 'I and thou' is a spiritual model for this ideal type of human relationship.

2 The cultural trap: the language of images

1 On stereotypes of the aged, see Bateson (1950), Stennett and Thurlow (1958), Lehr (1983), and Gruman (1978). For reflection on stereotype-riddled studies in gerontology, see Maddox (1969), Thomas (1981), and Manheimer (1990).
2 The concept of 'symbolic type' is an outgrowth of anthropological discussion of the splitting of the 'me' (the negotiated persona) from the 'I' (inner self), presenting inner as outer but still as non-negotiable and socially independent of context (see Grathoff 1970; Handelman and Kapferer 1980; Handelman 1991). A symbolic type is a reified cultural paradigm which, though itself independent of context, can shape it and, though itself closed to social negotiation and role interplay, has an impact on these processes. Symbolic types emerge when social order collapses, boundaries become blurred and elusive, and social action is no longer informed by corresponding cultural meaning.
3 This triple taboo – death, sex, and excrement – may be the core image in our attitude towards AIDS.

3 The personal trap: the language of self-presentation

1 Since I do not presume to delve into the inner selves of the aged, the only information at my disposal is that of observable behaviour. On the one hand, behaviour may be seen as a means by which feelings and cognitions may be deduced. On the other, self-presentation can be seen as a form of impression management and worthy of explanation in and of itself (Goffman 1959).

2 For an exposition of various dimensions of the holistic bio-psychosocial model in medicine, see Reiser and Rosen (1984).

4 The theoretical trap: the missing language

1 Moore (1978) developed the concepts of 'life term arena' and 'limited term arena' to distinguish between a life cycle within the same social context and a contextually fragmented life cycle.

7 Another universe: time, space, and self

1 The distinction between cultural codes and systems of social control has always been a major underpinning of anthropological thought. For example, the concept of 'two-dimensional man' developed by Cohen (1974) and the vectors of 'grid' and 'group' propounded by Douglas (1970, 1978, 1982) may be adduced as attempts to explore the relationship between these two realms of human life.

2 The various combinations in which means and ends are interlinked are analysed in Merton's (1963: chapters 18, 19) model of anomie.

3 The notion of the priority of form over substance has been developed along various theoretical lines. Simmel's work on 'social forms' could be regarded as heralding the general line of thought (for an example of special relevance to ageing see Simmel 1971). Goffman, whose arguments are to some extent thematic derivatives of Simmel's ideas, developed the thesis (see, e.g., Goffman 1974). In anthropology, Bateson is arguably the most intriguing contributor to this line of thought. His theory of the double-bind, schismogenesis, and schizophrenia (Bateson 1956) could be regarded as an important contribution to the understanding of the cultural position of the aged in Western society (see Teski 1983). The work of Victor Turner (1969) strikes a fine balance between structure and substance, and its emphasis on the stage of liminality in rites of passage has been acknowledged as a unique contribution to the understanding of ageing (see Myerhoff 1984; Hazan 1985). The possible contributions of structuralism and deconstructionism to the understanding of ageing have yet to be explored.

4 On the status of the aged as cultural strangers, see Dowd (1986). This outlook invokes the concept of invisibility, which has been used to

suggest the symbolic entropy of older people within their cultural milieu (see Myerhoff 1978a and Unruh 1983).

5 A number of ethnographic accounts support the plausibility of this proposal, particularly with regard to its egalitarian and communal elements (see, e.g., Keith 1982; Colson 1977; G. Becker 1980; Myerhoff 1978a; Hazan 1980a; Jerrome 1981, 1989). For an interesting anthropological comparison between retirement communities and African age-sets, see Legesse (1979). Clearly, not all old-age homogeneous settings conform to this social code, and many cases can be brought to illustrate the opposite, namely, competition and hierarchy (see, e.g., Handelman 1977 and Okely 1990). Other social organizations unrelated to old age possess similar characteristics (see, e.g., Woodburn 1981 on hunter-gatherers, Musgrove 1977 on the disabled, Miller and Gwynne 1972 on hospitals for the chronically sick, and Abrams and McCulloch 1976 on communes).

Conclusions

1 Since learning the metalanguage of ageing requires extensive structural knowledge of the culture in question, it would be advisable to follow Schneider's (1968) type of cultural analysis and explore the existential dilemmas in the light of which the symbolic codes of ageing are formulated. This avenue, together with the assumption that human behaviour is a product of human knowledge, leads us to Foucault (1972), whose thinking may further our understanding of the discourse of ageing.

Bibliography

Abel, E. K. (1987). *Love Is Not Enough: Family Care of the Frail Elderly*, Washington DC, American Public Health Association.

Abrams, P. and McCulloch, A. (1976). *Communes, Sociology and Society*, Cambridge, Cambridge University Press.

Alport, G. W. (1959). *The Structure of Prejudice*, Cambridge, MA, Addison-Wesley.

Altergott, K. (ed.) (1988). *Daily Life in Later Life: Comparative Perspectives*, Newbury Park, CA, Sage.

Amoss, P. T. and Harell, S. (1981a). 'Introduction: An anthropological perspective on aging', in P. T. Amoss and S. Harrell (eds.), *Other Ways of Growing Old: Anthropological Perspectives*, Stanford, CA, Stanford University Press, pp. 1–24.

(1981b). *Other Ways of Growing Old: Anthropological Perspectives*, Stanford, Stanford University Press.

Anderson, B. (1972). 'The process of deculturation: Its dynamics among United States aged', *Anthropological Quarterly*, 45, 209–16.

Ariès, P. (1965). *Centuries of Childhood*, New York, Vintage Books.

(1983). *The Hour of Our Death*, London, Penguin.

Atchley, R. C. (1977). *The Social Forces in Later Life*, Belmont, CA, Wadsworth.

(1979). 'Issues in retirement research', *Gerontologist*, 19, 14–54.

Atchley, R. C. and Miller, S. J. (1983). 'Types of elderly couples', in T. H. Brubaker (ed.). *Family Relationships in Later Life*, Beverly Hills, CA, Sage, pp. 77–90.

Baltes, P. B. and Schaie, K. W. (1977). 'Aging and I.Q.: The myth of the twilight years', in S. H. Zarit (ed.), *Readings in Aging and Death: Contemporary Perspectives*, New York, Harper & Row, pp. 67–71.

Barthes, R. (1977). *Image, Music, Text*, London, Fontana.

Bateson, G. (1950). 'Cultural ideas about aging', in H. E. Jones (ed.), *Proceedings of a Conference Held in August 7–10, 1950, at the University of California, Berkeley*, New York, Pacific Coast Committee on Old Age Research, Social Science Research Council.

Bibliography

(1956). 'Toward a theory of schizophrenia', *Behavioral Sciences*, 1, 251–64.

(1972). 'A theory of play and fantasy', in *Steps Towards an Ecology of Mind*, San Fransisco, Chandier.

Bauman, Z. (1992). *Mortality, Immortality and Other Life Strategies*, Cambridge, Polity Press.

Baxter, P. and Almagor, V. (1978). *Age, Generation, and Time*, New York, St. Martin's Press.

Baycreft Terrace Memoirs Group (1979). *From our Lives: Memories, Life Stories, Episodes and Recollections*, Ontario, Canada, Mosaic Press.

Becker, E. (1962). *The Birth and Death of Meaning*, New York, Free Press.

(1973). *The Denial of Death*, New York, Free Press.

Becker, G. (1980). *Growing Old in Silence*, Berkeley and Los Angeles, University of California Press.

Bellah, R. N., Sullivan, Swidler and Tipton (1985). *Habits of the Heart: Individualism and Commitment in American Life*, Berkeley, University of California Press.

Bengtson, V. L. (1979). 'Research perspectives on inter-generational interaction', in P. K. Ragan (ed.), *Aging Parents*, Berkeley and Los Angeles, University of California Press.

Bengtson, V. and Dowd, J. (1980). 'Sociological functionalism, exchange theory, and life cycle analysis: A call for more explicit theoretical bridges', *International Journal of Aging and Human Development*, 12, 55–73.

Bengtson, V. L. and Robertson, J. F. (eds.) (1985). *Grandparenthood*, Beverly Hills, CA, Sage Publications.

Berger, P. L. (1966). *Invitation to Sociology*, London, Penguin.

Berger, P., Berger, B. and Kellner, H. (1973). *The Homeless Mind*, New York, Random House.

Bernardi, B. (1985). *Age Class Systems: Social Institutions and Politics Based on Age*, Cambridge, Cambridge University Press.

Bernstein, B. (1971). *Class, Codes and Control*, London, Routledge & Kegan Paul.

Berry, R. J. (1981). 'The genetics of death: Mortal, morbid and selfish genes', in S. C. Humphreys and H. Kind (eds.), *Mortality and Immortality: The Anthropology and Archaeology of Death*, London, Academic Press, pp. 59–79.

Bertaux, D. (ed.) (1981). *Biography and Society: The Life History Approach in the Social Sciences*, London, Sage.

Binstock, R. H. and Shanas, E. (eds.) (1976). *Handbook of Aging and the Social Sciences*, New York, Von Nostrand Reinhold.

(eds.) (1985). *Handbook of Aging and the Social Sciences*, 2nd edn, New York, Van Nostrand Reinhold.

Birren, J. E. and Bengtson, V. I. (eds.) (1988). *Emergent Theories of Aging*, New York, Springer.

Birren, J. E. and Schaie, K. W. (1985). *Handbook of the Psychology of Aging*, 2nd edn, New York, Van Nostrand Reinhold.

Bloch, M. (1971). *Facing the Dead*, London, Academic Press.

Bloch, M. and Parry, J. (eds.) (1982). *Death and the Regeneration of Life*, Cambridge, Cambridge University Press.

Blythe, R. (1979). *The View in Winter*, London, Penguin.

Bonds, D. E. (1990). 'The separative self in Sylvia Plath's *The Bell Jar*', *Women Studies*, 18, 49–64.

Bouissac, P. (1976). *Circus and Culture*, Bloomington, Indiana University Press.

Bourdieu, P. (1984). *Distinctions*, Cambridge, MA, Harvard University Press.

Brubaker, T. H. (ed.) (1983). *Family Relationships in Later Life*, Beverly Hills, CA, Sage.

Buber, M. (1937). *I and Thou*, trans. R. G. Smith, Edinburgh. See also Schlipp, P. A. and Friedman, M. (1967). *The Philosophy of Martin Buber*, La Salle, IL.

Burgess, E. (1950). 'Personal and social adjustment in old age', in M. Derber (ed.), *The Aged and Society*, Champaign, IL, Industrial Relations Research Association, pp. 138–56.

Butler, R. N. (1969). 'Age-ism: Another form of bigotry', *Gerontologist*, 9, 243–6.

——— (1975). *Why Survive? Being Old in America*, New York, Harper & Row.

Byrne, S. W. and Arden, S. W. (1974). 'An adult community', in G. Foster and R. Kemper (eds.), *Anthropologists in Cities*, Boston, Little, Brown.

Cain, L. D., Jr. (1974). 'The growing importance of legal age in determining the status of the elderly', *Gerontologist*, 14, 167–74.

Clark, M. and Anderson, B. G. (1967). *Culture and Aging: An Anthropological Study of Older Americans*, Springfield, IL, Charles C. Thomas.

Clavan, S. (1978). 'The impact of social class and social trends on the role of grandparents', *Family Coordinator*, 27, 351–8.

Coe, R. (1965). 'Self-conception and institutionalization', in A. Rose and W. Peterson (eds.), *Older People and Their Social World*, Philadelphia, F. A. Davis.

Cohen, A. (1974). *Two-Dimensional Man*, London, Routledge & Kegan Paul.

Cohen, D. and Eisdorfer, C. (1986). *The Loss of Self*, New York, Norton.

Cole, T. R. and Gradow, S. A. (eds.) (1986). *What Does It Mean to Grow Old?* Durham, NC, Duke University Press.

Coleman, P. (1986). *Ageing and Reminiscence Processes*, Chichester, John Wiley.

Colson, E. (1977). 'The least common denominator', in S. F. Moore and B. Myerhoff (eds.), *Secular Ritual*, Assen, Van Gorcum, pp. 189–98.

Cool, L. and McCabe, J. (1983). '"The scheming hag" and the "dear old thing": The anthropology of ageing women', in J. Sokolovsky (ed.), *Growing Old in Different Societies*, Belmont, CA, Wadsworth, pp. 56–71.

Cooley, C. H. (1972). 'The looking glass self', in J. Manis and A. Meltzer (eds.), *Symbolic Interaction*, Boston, Allyn & Bacon, pp. 231–3.

Cowgill, D. and Holmes L. (eds.) (1972). *Aging and Modernization*, New York, Appleton-Century-Croft.

Cumming, G. E. and Henry W. W. (1961). *Growing Old: The Process of Disengagement*, New York, Basic Books.

(1976). 'Engagement with an old theory', *International Journal of Aging and Human Development*, 6, 187–91.

Cunningham-Burley, S. (1987). 'The experience of grandfatherhood', in C. Lewis and M. O'Brien (eds.), *Reassessing Fatherhood*, London, Sage.

de Beauvoir, S. (1975). *The Coming of Age*, New York, Warner Communication Co.

Dolgin, J. F. Kemnitzer, D. S. and Schneider, D. M. (1977). 'Introduction', in J. L. Dolgin, D. S. Kemnitzer and D. M. Schneider (eds.), *Symbolic Anthropology: A Reader in the Study of Symbols and Meaning*, New York, Columbia University Press.

Doob, L. (1971). *Patterning of Time*, New Haven, Yale University Press.

Dougherty, M. (1978). 'An anthropological perspective on aging and women in the middle years', in E. Bauwens (ed.), *The Anthropology of Health*, St. Louis, C. V. Mosby, pp. 177–91.

Douglas, M. (1966). *Purity and Danger*, New York, Pantheon Books.

(1970). *Natural Symbols: Explorations in Cosmology*, New York, Pantheon Books.

(1973). *Rules and Meanings*, London, Penguin.

(1978). *Cultural Bias*, London, Royal Anthropological Institute of Great Britain and Ireland.

(ed.) (1982). *Essays in the Sociology of Perception*, London, Routledge & Kegan Paul.

Douglas, M. and Isherwood, B. (1978). *The World of Goods*, New York, Basic Books.

Dowd, J. J. (1975). 'Aging as exchange: A preface to theory', *Journal of Gerontology*, 30, 584–94.

(1978). 'Aging as exchange: A test of the distributive justice proposition', *Pacific Sociological Review*, 21, 351–75.

(1980). *Stratification among the Aged*, Monterey, CA, Brooks/Cole.

(1986). 'The old person as stranger', in V. W. Marshall (ed.), *Later Life: The Social Psychology of Aging*, Beverly Hills, CA, Sage, pp. 147–90.

Eckert, J. K. (1980). *The Unseen Elderly*, San Diego, CA, Campanile Press.

Elder, G. H., Jr. (1974). *Children of the Great Depression*, Chicago, University of Chicago Press.

Eliade, M. (1967). *Death, Afterlife, and Eschatology*, New York, Harper & Row.

Elias, N. (1985). *The Loneliness of the Dying*, Oxford, Basil Blackwell.

Erikson, E. (1950). *Childhood and Society*, New York, Norton.

Esberger, K. (1978). 'Body image', *Journal of Gerontological Nursing*, 4, 35–8.

Espenshade, T. J. and Braun, R. E. (1983). 'Economic aspects of an aging population and the material well-being of older persons', in M. White Riley, B. B. Hess, and K. Bond (eds.), *Aging in Society: Selected Reviews of Recent Research*, Hillsdale, NJ, Lawrence Erlbaum Association, pp. 25–52.

Estes, D. L. (1979). *The Aging Enterprise*, San Francisco, Jossey-Bass.

Evans-Pritchard, E. E. (1939). 'Nuer time reckoning', *Africa*, 16, 189–216.

Ewing, K. P. (1900). 'The illusion of wholeness: Culture, self, and the experience of inconsistency', *Ethos*, 215–78.

Fabian, J. (1983). *Time and the Other: How Anthropology Makes Its Object*, New York, Columbia University Press.

Featherstone, M. and Hepworth, M. (1991). 'The mask of ageing and the postmodern life course', in M. Featherstone, M. Hepworth and B. Turner (eds.), *The Body: Social Process and Cultural Theory*, London, Sage, pp. 370–89.

Fischer, D. H. (1978). *Growing Old in America*, expanded edn, New York, Oxford University Press.

Fisher, W. R. (1987). *Human Communication as Narration: Toward a Philosophy of Reason, Value, and Action*, Columbia, University of South Carolina Press.

Foner, N. (1984). *Ages in Conflict: A Cross-Cultural Perspective on Inequality between Old and Young*, New York, Columbia University Press.

Fontana, A. (1976). *The Lost Frontier*, Beverly Hills, CA, Sage.

Foucault, M. (1972). *The Archaeology of Knowledge*, New York, Pantheon Books.

(1978). *The History of Sexuality*, New York, Pantheon Books.

Francis, D. (1984). *Will You Still Need Me, Will You Still Feed Me, When I'm 84?* Bloomington, IN, Indiana University Press.

Frank, G. and Vanderburgh, R. M. (1986). 'Cross-cultural use of life history methods in gerontology', in J. Keith and contributors. *New Methods for Old Age Research: Strategies for Studying Diversity*, South Hadley, MA, Bergin & Garvey, pp. 185–212.

Freuchen, P. (1961). *Book of the Eskimos*, Greenwich, CT, Fawcett Crest Book.

Fry, C. (ed.) (1980). *Aging in Culture and Society: Comparative Viewpoints and Strategies*, New York, J. F. Bergin.

(1981). *Dimensions: Aging, Culture, and Health*, New York, J. F. Bergin.

Garfinkel, H. (1967a). *Studies in Ethnomethodology*, Englewood Cliffs, NJ, Prentice-Hall.

(1967b). 'Passing and the managed achievement of sex status in an intersexed person', in H. Garfinkel, *Studies in Ethnomethodology*, Englewood Cliffs, NJ, Prentice-Hall, pp. 116–85.

Geertz, C. (1979). 'From the native's point of view: On the nature of anthropological understanding', in P. Rabinow and W. N. Sullivan (eds.), *Interpretive Social Science: A Reader*, Berkeley and Los Angeles, University of California Press, pp. 225–41.

Gellner, E. (1973). *Cause and Meaning in The Social Sciences*, London: Routledge and Kegan Paul.

George, L. (1979). 'The happiness syndrome: Methodological and substantive issues in the study of social-psychological well-being in adulthood, *Gerontologist*, 10, 210–16.

(1980). *Role Transitions in Later Life*, Monterey, CA, Brooks/Cole.

Gergen, K. J. and Back, K. W. (1966). 'Aging and the paradox of somatic concern', in I. H. Simpson and J. O. Kinney (eds.), *Social Aspects of Aging*, Durham, NC, Duke University Press, pp. 306–21.

Giddens, A. (1991). *Modernity and Self-Identity: Self and Society in the Late Modern Age*, Cambridge, Polity Press.

Glascock, A. P. and Feinman, S. L. (1980), 'Toward a comparative framework: Propositions concerning the treatment of the aged in nonindustrial societies', in C. L. Fry and J. Keith (eds.), *New Methods for Old Age Research*, Chicago, Loyola University Center for Urban Policy.

(1981). 'Social asset or social burden: Treatment of the aged in nonindustrial societies', in C. L. Fry (ed.), *Dimensions: Aging, Culture, and Health*, New York, J. F. Bergin, pp. 13–32.

Goffman, E. (1959). *The Presentation of Self in Everyday Life*, New York, Doubleday.

(1961). *Asylums*, New York, Doubleday.

(1963). *Stigma: Notes on the Management of Spoiled Identity*, Englewood Cliffs, NJ, Prentice-Hall.

(1974). *Frame Analysis*, New York, Harper.

Goody, J. (1976). 'Aging in non-industrial societies', in R. H. Binstock and E. Shanas (eds.), *Handbook of Aging and the Social Sciences*, New York, Van Nostrand Reinhold, pp. 117–29.

(1979). *The Domestication of the Savage Mind*, Cambridge, Cambridge University Press.

Gordon, B. J. (1975). 'A disengaged look at disengagement theory', *International Journal of Aging and Human Development*, 6, 215–27.

Graburn, N. H. H. (1969). *Eskimos without Igloos*, Boston, Little, Brown.

Graehner, W. (1980). *History of Retirement*, New Haven, Yale University Press.

Grathoff, R. (1970). *The Structure of Social Inconsistencies*, The Hague, Nijhoff.

Gruman, G. J. (1978). 'Cultural origins of present-day "ageism": The modernization of the life-cycle', in F. Woodward, M. Kathleen Van Tassell, and D. Van Tassell (eds.), *Aging and the Elderly: Humanistic Perspectives in Gerontology*, Atlantic Highlands, NJ. Humanities Press.

Gubrium, J. F. (1972). 'Toward a socio-environmental theory of aging', *Gerontologist*, 12, 281–4.

(1975). *Living and Dying at Murray Manor*, New York, St. Martin's Press.

(1986). *Oldtimers and Alzheimer's: The Descriptive Organization of Senility*, Greenwich, CT, JAI Press.

Gubrium, J. F. and Lynott, R. S. (1983). 'Rethinking life satisfaction', *Human Organization*, 42, 30–8.

Guillemard, A. M. (ed.) (1983). *Old Age and the Welfare State*, Beverly Hills, CA, Sage.

Gusfield, J. (1981). *The Culture of Public Problems: Drinking, Driving, and Their Symbolic Order*, Chicago, University of Chicago Press.

Hall, E. T. (1984). *The Dance of Life: The Other Dimension of Time*, New York, Doubleday/Anchor.

Hallowell, I. (1937). 'Temporal orientations in Western civilization and in pre-literate society', *American Anthropologist*, 39, 649–70.

Handelman, D. (1977). *Work and Play among the Aged*, Amsterdam, Van Gorcum.

—— (1981). 'The ritual clown: Attributes and affinities', *Anthropos*, 76, 321–70.

—— (1990). *Models and Mirrors*, Cambridge, Cambridge University Press.

—— (1991). 'Symbolic types, the body, and circus', *Semiotica*, 85, (3–4): 205–27

Handelman, D. and Kapferer, B. (1980). 'Symbolic types, mediation and the transformation of ritual context: Sinhalese demons and Tewa clowns', *Semiotica*, 30, 41–71.

Hareven, T. K. (1978). 'Cycles, courses, and cohorts: Reflections on theoretical and methodological approaches to the historical study of family development', *Journal of Social History*, 12, 97–110.

—— (1981). 'Historical changes in the timing of family transitions: Their impact on generational relations'., in R. W. Fogel (ed.), *Aging: Stability and Change in the Family*, New York, Academic Press, pp. 143–65.

Hareven, T. K. and Adams, K. J. (eds.) (1982). *Ageing and Life Course Transitions: An Interdisciplinary Perspective*, London, Tavistock.

Harris, A. J. and Fineberg, J. (1978). 'Television and aging: Is what you see what you get?', *Gerontologist*, 18, 484–8.

Havighurst, R. J. (1954). 'Flexibility and social roles of the aged', *American Journal of Sociology*, 98, 309–13.

—— (1963). 'Successful aging', in R. H. Williams, C. Tibbitts, and W. Donahue (eds.), *Processing of Aging*, vol. I, New York, Atherton Press.

—— (1975). 'The future aged: The use of time and money', *Gerontologist*, 15, 10–15.

Havighurst, R., Neugarten, B. and Tobin, S. (1968). 'Disengagement and patterns of aging', in B. Neugarten (ed.), *Middle Age and Aging*, Chicago, The University of Chicago Press, pp. 161–72.

Hazan, H. (1980a). *The Limbo People: A Study of the Constitution of the Time Universe among the Aged*, London, Routledge & Kegan Paul.

—— (1980b). 'Adjustment and control in an old age home', in E. Marx (ed.)., *A Composite Portrait of Israel*, London, Academic Press.

—— (1981). 'Totality as an adaptive strategy: Two case studies of the management of powerlessness', *Social Analysis*, 2, 63–76,

—— (1983). 'Discontinuity and identity: A case study of social reintegration among the aged', *Research on Aging*, 5, 473–89.

—— (1984). 'Religion in an old age home: Symbolic adaptation as a survival strategy', *Ageing and Society*, 4:137–56.

—— (1985). 'Continuity and transformation among the aged: A study in the anthropology of time', *Current Anthropology*, 35, 367–78.

—— (1987a). 'Myth into reality: Enacting life histories in an institutional setting', in G. L. Maddox and E. W. Busse (eds.), *Aging: The Universal Human Experience*, New York, Springer, pp. 441–50).

(1987b). 'Holding time still with cups of tea', in M. Douglas (ed.), *Constructive Drinking*, Cambridge, Cambridge University Press, pp. 205–19.

(1990). 'Victim into sacrifice: The construction of the old as a symbolic type', *Journal of Cross-Cultural Gerontology*, 5, 77–84.

Heintz, K. (1976). *Retirement Communities: For Adults Only*, New York, Macmillan.

Hendricks, J. and Hendricks, C. D. (1977). 'Sexuality in later life', in *Aging in Mass Society*, Cambridge, MA, Winthrop, pp. 304–11. Reprinted in V. Carver and P. Lippiard (eds.), *An Ageing Population*, Sevenoaks, Kent, Hodder & Stoughton, pp. 64–71.

Henry, J. (1963). *Culture against Man*, New York, Random House.

Henry, W. E. (1964). 'The theory of intrinsic disengagement', in P. F. Hansen (ed.), *Age with a Future*, Philadelphia, F. A. Davis.

Hertz, R. (1960 [1928]). *Death and the Right Hand*, London, Routledge & Kegan Paul,

Hess, B. B. and Markson, E. W. (1980). *Aging and Old Age: An Introduction to Social Gerontology*, New York, Macmillan, pp. 231–6.

Hochschild, A. R. (1973). *The Unexpected Community*, Englewood Cliffs, NJ, Prentice-Hall.

(1975). 'Disengagement theory: A critique and proposal', *American Sociological Review*, 40, 553–69.

(1983). *The Managed Heart*, Berkeley and Los Angeles, University of California Press.

Holy, L. and Stucklik, M. (1983). *Actions, Norms and Representations*, Cambridge, Cambridge University Press.

Jacobs, J. (1974). *Fun City: An Ethnographic Study of a Retirement Community*, New York, Holt, Rinehart & Winston.

(1975). *Older Persons and Retirement Communities: Case Studies in Social Gerontology*, Springfield, IL, Charles C. Thomas.

Jerrome, D. (1981). 'The significance of friendship for women in later life', *Ageing and Society*, 1, 175–97.

(1989). 'Virtue and vicissitude: The social construction of old age in selected old age organizations', in M. Jeffrey (ed.), *As Britain Ages*, London, Routledge & Kegan Paul, pp. 151–65.

Johnson, M. L. (1976). 'That was your life: A biographical approach to later life', in J. M. A. Munnichs and W. Van den Heuvel (eds.), *Dependency or Interdependency in Old Age*, The Hague, Nijhoff.

Johnson, S. K. (1971). *Idle Haven: Community Building Among the Working Class Retired*, Berkeley, University of California Press.

Kalish, R. A. (1972). 'Of social values and the dying: A defence of disengagement', *Family Coordinator*, 21, 81–94.

(1976). 'Death and dying in a social context', in R. H. Binstock and E. Shanas (eds.), *Handbook of Aging and the Social Sciences*, New York, Van Nostrand Reinhold, pp. 483–507.

Kalish, R. A. and Knudtson, F. W. (1976). 'Attachment vs. disengagement: A life-span conceptualization', *Human Development*, 19, 171–81.

Kastenbaum, R. J. (1977). *Death, Society, and Human Experience*, St. Louis, C. V. Mosby.

Katz, S. H. (1978). 'Anthropological perspectives on aging', *Annals of the American Academy of Political and Social Sciences*, 438, 1–12.

Kaufman, S. 'Cultural components of identity in old age', *Ethos*, 9, 51–87.

(1986). *The Ageless Self: Sources of Meaning in Later Life*, Madison, University of Wisconsin Press.

Keith, J. (1980a). 'Old age and community creation', in C. L. Fry (ed.), *Aging in Culture and Society*, New York, J. F. Bergin, pp. 170–97.

(1980b). 'The best is yet to be: Toward an anthropology of age', *Annual Review of Anthropology*, 9, 339–64.

(1982). *Old People, New Lives*, Chicago, University of Chicago Press.

Keith, J. and contributors (1986). *New Methods for Old Age Research: Strategies for Studying Diversity*, South Hadley, MA, Bergin & Garvey.

Kertzer, D. and Keith J. (eds.) (1984). *Age and Anthropological Theory*, Ithaca, Cornell University Press.

Kivnick, H. (1982). 'Grandparenthood: An overview of meaning and mental health', *Gerontologist*, 22, 59–66.

Klemm, D. E. (1983). *The Hermeneutical Theory of Paul Ricoeur*, Lewisberg, PA, Bucknell University Press.

Kluckhohn, F. (1950). 'Dominant and substitute profiles of cultural orientations: Their significance for the analysis of social stratification', *Social Forces*, 218, 376–3.

Kreps, J. M. (1976). 'The economy and the aged', in R. H. Binstock, and E. Shanas (eds.), *Handbook of Aging and the Social Sciences*, New York, Van Nostrand Reinhold, pp. 272–85.

Kristeva, J. (1980). *Desire in Language: A Semiotic Approach to Literature and Art*, New York, Columbia University Press.

Kuper, A. (1988). *The Invention of Primitive Society*, London, Routledge & Kegan Paul.

Lakoff, G. and Johnson, M. (1980). *Metaphors We Live By*, Chicago, University of Chicago Press.

Langness, L. L., and Frank, G. (1981). *Lives: An Anthropological Approach to Biography*, Novato, CA, Chandler & Sharp.

Lasch, C. (1979). *The Culture of Narcissism: American Life in an Age of Diminishing Expectations*, New York, Warner Books.

Laslett, P. (1989). *A Fresh Map of Life: The Emergence of the Third Age*, London, Weidenfeld & Nicolson.

Lavie, S. (1990). *The Poetics of Military Occupation*, Berkeley and Los Angeles, University of California Press.

Leach, E. (1971). 'Chronics and chronos', in *Rethinking Anthropology*, London, Athlone Press, pp. 124–32.

(1976). *Culture and Communication: The Logic by which Symbols Are Connected*, Cambridge, Cambridge University Press.

Legesse, A. (1979). 'Age sets and retirement communities', *Anthropological Quarterly*, 52, (1):61–9.

Lehr, U. (1983). 'Stereotypes of aging and age norms', in J. A. Birren, J. M. A. Munnichs, H. Thomae and M. Marvis (eds.), *Aging: A Challenge to Science and Society, vol. III, Behavioural Sciences and Conclusions*, Oxford, Oxford University Press, pp. 101–12.

Lévi-Strauss, C. (1967). *The Savage Mind*, Chicago, University of Chicago Press.

Levy, S. (1979). 'Temporal experience in the aged: Body integrity and the social milieu', *International Journal of Aging and Human Development*, 9, 316–44.

Lieberman, M. A. and Tobin, S. S. (1983). *The Experience of Old Age: Stress, Coping, and Survival*, New York, Basic Books.

Lifton, R. J. (1977). 'The sense of immortality', in H. Feifel (ed.), *New Meanings of Death*, New York, McGraw-Hill.

(1983). *The Broken Connection*, New York, Basic Books.

(1986). *The Nazi Doctors*, New York, Basic Books.

Lopata, H. Z. (1983). 'Widowhood: Social norms and social integration', in J. A. Birren, J. M. A. Munnichs, H. Thomae and M. Marvis (eds.), *Aging: A Challenge to Science and Society, vol. III, Behavioural Sciences and Conclusions*, Oxford, Oxford University Press, pp. 155–69.

Luckmann, B. (1970). 'The small life worlds of modern man', *Social Research*, 37, 580–96.

Luscher, K. (1974). '"Time": A much neglected dimension in social theory and research', *Sociological Analysis and Theory*, 4, 101–17.

McCulloch, A. W. (1980). 'What do we mean by "development" in old age?', *Ageing and Society*, 1, 230–45.

McKee, P. L. (ed.) (1982). *Philosophical Foundations of Gerontology*, New York, Human Sciences Press.

Maddox, G. L. (1964). 'Disengagement theory: A critical evaluation', *Gerontologist*, 4, 80–72.

(1969). 'Growing old: Getting beyond the stereotypes', in Boyd and Oakes (eds.), *Foundations of Practical Gerontology*, Columbia, University of South Carolina Press, pp. 5–16.

Manheimer, R. (1990). 'The narrative quest in qualitative gerontology', *Journal of Aging Studies*, 3, 253–62.

Marshall, V. W. (1979). 'No exit: A symbolic interactionist perspective on aging', *International Journal of Aging and Human Development*, 9, 345–58.

Mason, H. (1980). 'Myth as an "ambush" to reality', in A. M. Olson (ed.), *Myth, Symbol, and Reality*, Notre Dame, University of Notre Dame Press, pp. 15–19.

Matthews, S. H . (1979). *The Social World of Old Women*, Beverly Hills, CA, Sage.

Maxwell, R. J. (1972). 'Anthropological perspectives', in H. Yaker, H. Damond and F. Cheek (eds.), *The Future of Time*, New York, Anchor Books, p. 36–72.

Maxwell, R. and Silverman, P. (1970). 'Information and esteem: Cultural considerations in the treatment of the aged', *Aging and Human Development*, 1, 361–92.

Mead, G. H. (1934). *Mind, Self, and Society*, Chicago, University of Chicago Press.

Merton, R. K. (1963). *Social Theory and Social Structure*, Glencoe, Free Press.

Midwinter, E. (1982). *Age Is Opportunity: Education and Older People*, London, Centre for Policy on Ageing.

(ed.) (1984). *Mutual Aid Universities*, London, Croom Helm.

Miller, A. (1973). 'Ends, means and galumphing', *American Anthropologist*, (75): 87–97.

Miller, E. J. and Gwynne, G. V. (1972). *A Life Apart*, London, Tavistock.

Moore, S. F. (1978). 'Old age in a life-term social arena: Some Chagga of Kilimanjaro in 1974', in B. Myerhoff and A. Simic (eds.), *Life's Career – Aging: Cultural Variations on Growing Old*, Beverly Hills, CA, Sage, pp. 23–76.

Morris, R. and Bass, S. A. (eds.) (1988). *Retirement Reconsidered: Economic and Social Roles for Older People*, New York, Springer.

Musgrove, F. (1977). 'A home for the disabled: A change of tense', in *Margins of the Mind*, London, Methuen, pp. 86–108.

Myerhoff, B. (1978a). *Number Our Days*, New York, Dutton.

(1978b). 'A symbol perfected in death: Continuity and ritual in the life and death of an elderly Jew', in B. Myerhoff and A. Simic (eds.), *Life's Career – Aging: Cultural Variations on Growing Old*, Beverly Hills, CA, Sage, pp. 163–206.

(1982). 'Life history among the elderly: Performance, visibility, and remembering', in J. Ruby (ed.), *A Crack in the Mirror: Reflexive Perspectives in Anthropology*, Philadelphia, University of Pennsylvania Press, pp. 99–120.

(1984). 'Rites and signs of ripening: The intertwining of ritual, time, and growing older', in D. L. Kertzer and J. Keith (eds.), *Age and Anthropological Theory*, Ithaca, Cornall University Press, pp. 305–30.

Myerhoff, B. and Simic, A. (eds.), (1978). *Life's Career – Aging: Cultural Variations on Growing Old*, Beverly Hills, CA, Sage.

Myerhoff, B. and Tufte, V. (1975). 'Life history as integration: Personal myth and aging', *Gerontologist*, 15, 541–3.

Neugarten, B. L. (1975). 'The future and the young-old', *Gerontologist*, 15, 4–9.

(1977). 'Personality and the aging process', in S. H. Zarit (ed.), *Readings in Aging and Death: Contemporary Perspectives*, New York, Harper & Row, pp. 72–7.

117

Okely, J. (1990), 'Clubs for Le Troisieme Age Communitas or Conflict', in P. Spencer (ed.), *Anthropology and the Riddle of the Sphinx*, London, Routledge, pp. 194–212.

Orbach, H. (1973). 'Disengagement activity controversy: Underlying theoretical models of aging', *Gerontologist*, 13, 72.

Palgi, P. and Abramovitz, H. (1985). 'Death from a cross-cultural perspective', *Annual Review of Anthropology*, 13, 385–417.

Palmore, E. (1975). *The Honourable Elders: A Cross-Cultural Analysis of Aging in Japan*, Durham, NC, Duke University Press.

Palmore E. and Manton, K. (1973). 'Ageism compared to racism and sexism', *Journal of Gerontology*, 38, 353–69.

Pearlin, L. and Schooler, C. (1978). 'The structure of coping', *Journal of Health and Social Behavior*, 19, 2–21.

Philibert, M. (1982). 'The phenomenological approaches to images of aging', in P. L. McKee (ed.), *Philosophical Foundations of Gerontology*, New York, Human Sciences Press, pp. 303–22.

Phillipson, C. (1982). *Capitalism and the Construction of Old Age*, London, Macmillan.

Plath, D. W. (1980). *Long Engagements: Maturity in Modern Japan*, Stanford, CA, Stanford University Press.

Porter, L. and Porter, L. (eds.) (1984). *Aging in Literature*, Troy, MI International Book Center.

Reinharz, S. and Rowles, D. (eds.) (1988). *Qualitative Gerontology*, New York, Springer.

Reiser, D. and Rosen D. H. (eds.) (1984). *Medicine as a Human Experience*, Baltimore, University Park Press.

Riley, M. W. (1979). 'Aging, social change, and social policy', in M. White Riley (ed.), *Aging from Birth to Death: Interdisciplinary Perspectives*, Washington, DC, American Association for the Advancement of Science.

Riley, M. W., Johnson, J. and Foner, A. (eds.) (1972). *Aging and Society, vol. III, A Sociology of Age Stratification*, New York, Russell Sage Foundation.

Roebuck, J. (1976). 'When does old age begin? The evolution of the English definition', *Journal of Social History*, 12, 416–28.

Rose, A. (1965). 'The subculture of the aging', in A. N. Rose and W. K. Peterson (eds.), *Older People and Their Social World*, Philadelphia, PA, Davis.

Rose, A. M. and Peterson, W. A. (eds.) (1965). *Older People and Their Social World: The Sub-Culture of Aging*, Philadelphia, F. A. Davis.

Rosenmayr, L. (1981). 'Age, lifespan and biography', *Ageing and Society*, 1, 29–49.

Rosow, I. (1974). *Socialization to Old Age*, Berkeley and Los Angeles, University of California Press.

Roth, J. (1962). *Timetables*, Indianapolis, IN, Bobbs-Merrill.

Rowles, G. D. (1978). *Prisoners of Space?* Boulder, CO, Westview Press.

Rowles, G. D. and Ohta, R. J. (1981). *Aging and Milieu*, New York, Academic Press.

Roy, D. (1959). 'Banana time: Job satisfaction and informal interaction', *Human Organization*, 18, 158–68.

Savishinsky, J. S. (1985). 'Pets and family relationships among nursing homes residents', *Marriage and Family Review*, 8, 109–34.

Schneider, D. (1968). *American Kinship: A Cultural Account*, Englewood Cliffs, NJ, Prentice-Hall.

Schultz, J. (1980). *The Economics of Aging*, Belmont, CA, Wadsworth.

Schutz, A. and Luckmann, T. (1973). *The Structure of the Life World*, Evanston, IL, Northwestern University Press.

Sheehy, G. (1976). *Passages: Predictable Crises of Adult Life*, London, Bantam Books.

Sheleff, L. S. (1981). *Generations Apart: Adult Hostility to Youth*, New York, McGraw-Hill.

Shotter, J. and Gergen, K. J. (eds.) (1980). *Texts of Identity*, London, Sage.

Shweder, R. A. and Levine, R. A. (eds.) (1984). *Culture Theory: Essays on Mind, Self and Emotion*, Cambridge, Cambridge University Press.

Sill, J. (1980). 'Disengagement reconsidered: Awareness of finitude', *Gerontologist*, 20, 457–62.

Simmel, G. (1971). 'The stranger', in D. N. Levine (ed.), *George Simmel on Individuality and Social Forms*, Chicago, University of Chicago Press, pp. 143–9.

Simmons, L. W. (1945). *The Role of the Aged in Primitive Society*, New Haven, Archon Books.

(1960). 'Aging in pre-industrial societies', in C. Tibbitts (ed.), *Handbook of Social Gerontology*, Chicago, University of Chicago Press.

Smith-Blau, Z. (1973). *Old Age in a Changing Society*, New York, New Viewpoints.

Sokolovsky, J. (ed.) (1983). *Growing Old in Different Societies*, Belmont, CA, Wadsworth.

(ed.) (1990). *The Cultural Context of Aging: Worldwide Perspectives*, Westport, CT: Bergin & Garvey.

Sontag, S. (1989). *AIDS and Its Metaphors*, New York, Farrar, Straus & Giroux.

Sperber, D. (1975). *Rethinking Symbolism*, Cambridge, Cambridge University Press.

Steiner, F. (1956). *Taboo*, London, Cohen & West.

Stennett, R. and Thurlow, M. (1958). 'Cultural symbolism: The age variable', *Journal of Consulting Psychology*, 22, 496.

Steward, F. (1976). *Fundamentals of Age-Group Systems*, New York, Academic Press.

Stone, G. P. (1970). 'Sex and age as universes of appearance', in G. P. Stone and A. Fargerman (eds.), *Social Psychology through Symbolic Interaction*, Waltham, MA, Xerox College Publishing, pp. 227–35.

Strathern, M. (1987). 'Out of context: The persuasive fictions of anthropology', *Current Anthropology*, 28, 251–81.

Strauss, A. (1978a). 'A social world perspective', in N. K. Denzin (ed.), *Studies in Symbolic Interaction*, vol. I, Greenwich, CT, JAI Press, pp. 119–28.

(1978b). *Negotiation*, San Francisco, Jossey-Bass.

Streib, G. F. (1965). 'Are the aged a minority group?', in A. Gouldner and S. M. Miller (eds.), *Applied Sociology*, New York, Free Press.

Sudnow, D. (1967). *Passing On: The Social Organization of Dying*, Englewood Cliffs, NJ, Prentice-Hall.

Sumner, W. G. (1940). *Folkways*, New York, New American Library.

Talmon-Garber, Y. (1962). 'Aging in collective settlements in Israel', in C. Tibbits and W. Donahue (eds.), *Aging around the World*, New York, Columbia University Press, pp. 426–41.

Taylor, M. K. (1985). 'Symbolic dimensions in cultural anthropology', *Current Anthropology*, 26, 167–86.

Teski, M. (1979a). *Living Together*, Washington DC, University Press of America.

(1979b). 'Aging, society, and progress', in B. T. Grindal and D. M. Warren (eds.), *Essays in Humanistic Anthropology: A Festschrift in Honor of David Bidney*, Washington, DC, University Press of America, pp. 219–33.

(1983). 'The evolution of aging, ecology, and the elderly in the modern world', in J. Sokolovsky (ed.), *Growing Old in Different Cultures*, Belmont, CA, Wadsworth, pp. 14–23.

Thomae, H. (1970). 'Theory of aging and cognitive theory of personality', *Human Development*, 13, 1–16.

Thomas, W. C. (1981). 'The expectation gap and the stereotype of the stereotype: Images of old people', *Gerontologist*, 21, 402–7.

Townsend, P. (1957). *The Family Life of Old People*, London, Routledge & Kegan Paul.

(1962). *The Last Refuge*, London, Routledge & Kegan Paul.

Turnbull, C. M. (1984). *The Human Cycle*, London, Jonathan Cape.

Turner, B. (1984). *The Body and Society: Explanations in Social Theory*, Oxford, Basil Blackwell.

Turner, V. (1969). *The Ritual Process: Structure and Anti-Structure*, Chicago, Aldine.

Turnstall, J. (1966). *Old and Alone*, London, Routledge & Kegan Paul.

University of the Third Age in Cambridge (1984). *The Image of the Elderly on TV*, Research Report no. 1, Cambridge, University of the Third Age in Cambridge.

Unruh, D. R. (1983). *Invisible Lives: Social Worlds of the Aged*, Beverly Hills, CA, Sage.

Van Gennep, A. (1969 [1908]). *The Rites of Passage*, trans. M. B. Visedom and G. L. Caffee, Chicago, Phoenix Books.

Vesperi, M. (1980). 'The reluctant consumer: Nursing home residents in the post-Bergman era', *Practicing Anthropology*, 3, 23–4, 70–8.

Wells, L. E. and S. Stryker (1988). 'Stability and change in Self over the life course', in P. B. Baltes, D. L. Featherman and R. M. Lerner (eds.), *Life-Span Development and Behavior*, 8: 191–224.

Wenger, C. (1984). *The Supportive Network*, London, George Allen & Unwin.

Werner, D. (1981). 'Gerontocracy among the Mekranoti of Central Brazil', *Anthropological Quarterly*, 54, 15–27.

Wilson, E. O. (1975). *Sociobiology: The New Synthesis*, Cambridge, MA, Harvard University Press.

Wilson, M. (1951). *Good Company: A Study of Nyakyusa Age Villages*, London, Oxford University Press.

Woodburn, J. (1981). 'Egalitarian societies', *Man*, 17, 431–51.

Woodward, K. M. & Schwarz, M. M. (eds.) (1988). *Memory and Desire: Aging – Literature – Psychoanalysis*, Bloomington, Indiana University Press.

Zarit, S. H. (ed.) (1977). *Readings in Aging and Death: Contemporary Perspectives*, New York, Harper & Row.

Zerubavel, E. (1982). *Hidden Rhythms*, Chicago, University of Chicago Press.
  (1985). *The Seven-Day Circle*, New York, Free Press.

Zimring, F. M. (1988). 'Attaining mastery: The shift from the "me" to the "I"', *Person-Centered Review*, 3, 165–75.

Index